PRAISE FOR *SMART PROSPECTING T*

Smart Prospecting is your new go-to sales [...] traditional techniques with a modern approach, following Mike's step-by-step process will amplify your success as a sales professional.
—Jeffrey Hayzlett, global business celebrity and bestselling author of *Running the Gauntlet* and *The Mirror Test*

In *Smart Prospecting* Mike Krause introduces a process that marries tried-and-true prospecting methods with today's cutting-edge tools and technology. Follow his process and you'll quickly fill your pipeline with qualified prospects and your pockets with bigger commission checks.
—Jeb Blount, CEO of SalesGravy.com and author of *People Buy YOU*

The prospecting game has changed and few are playing it well. Mike Krause provides the prospecting success secrets in today's business environment in *Smart Prospecting*. Don't just read the book. Absorb every word!
—Lee B. Salz, Sales Management Strategist, Sales Architects

If you have to prospect or cold call for a living, then make sure you have Mike's *Smart Prospecting* next to your phone. It is packed with up-to-date tips, shortcuts, and real-world scripts and techniques that will help you connect with and earn business from decision makers. An excellent resource you'll use over and over again!
—Mike Brooks, author of *The Ultimate Book of Phone Scripts*, www.MrInsideSales.com

In Krause's new book, *Smart Prospecting*, you will learn everything you need to know about targeting the right clientele for your business. The book is a must-read for entrepreneurs and salespeople motivated to succeed.
—Elinor Stutz, inspirational speaker, CEO, and author of *Nice Girls DO Get the Sale: Relationship Building That Gets Results*

Smart Prospecting is one of the most complete books written on the topic of sales prospecting. Michael Krause provides an abundance of examples of how to use different media. Novice and veteran salespeople will benefit from the insights contained in this book.
—Kelley Robertson, sales trainer, keynote speaker, and author of *The Secrets of Power Selling*

Smart Prospecting That Works Every Time! is the ideal book for entrepreneurs, salespeople, and want-to-bes. Time is our most valuable asset and Mike shows us how to prospect smarter, not harder, in less time. This is good R.O.T.I. (return on time invested).
—Bob Urichuck, ranked #4 in the World's Top 30 Sales Gurus, author of *Up Your Bottom Line*

Nothing happens in the sale until you can reach a decision maker, and this book will show you how. I've read nearly every book on the topic of prospecting and this one is at the top of my list.
—Jake Atwood, President, Ovation Sales Group

Mike takes the unlimited number of things you *could do* for prospecting and simplifies it so you know exactly what *to do* starting now. This book *is* your new prospecting plan! Read, learn, and absorb this book before your competitors do. BUY IT NOW!
—Erik Luhrs, author of *Be Do Sale* and creator of the GURUS Selling System

Mike's approach will give you a better, Smarter approach to prospecting. Read it, apply it, and you'll actually find yourself looking forward to prospecting.
—S. Anthony Iannarino, www.thesalesblog.com

Mike's powerful approach enables you to connect with your prospects deeply, to understand how to stand in their shoes, and to become a trusted advisor. One book—one perfect solution for all sales professionals!
—Judith E. Glaser, bestselling author of *Creating WE*, Chairman of the Creating WE Institute, www.creatingwe.com

Mike Krause takes away the smoke and mirrors, leaving both experienced and new salespeople with practical, easy-to-adopt lessons that help anyone learn to sell more effectively.
—Wendy Weiss, The Queen of Cold Calling™, www.wendyweiss.com

Smart Prospecting That Works Every Time!

Smart Prospecting That Works Every Time!

Win More Clients with Fewer Cold Calls

MICHAEL D. KRAUSE

Mc
Graw
Hill
Education

New York   Chicago   San Francisco   Athens   London   Madrid
Mexico City   Milan   New Delhi   Singapore   Sydney   Toronto

1 2 3 4 5 6 7 8 9 0   QFR/QFR   1 8 7 6 5 4 3

ISBN   978-0-07-180542-1
MHID 0-07-180542-7

e-ISBN   978-0-07-180543-8
e-MHID 0-07-180543-5

McGraw-Hill Education books are available at special quantity discounts to use as premiums and sales promotions or for use in corporate training programs. To contact a representative, please e-mail us at bulksales@mcgraw-hill.com.

This book is printed on acid-free paper.

Library of Congress Cataloging-in-Publication Data
Krause, Michael D.
    Smart prospecting that works every time! : win more clients with fewer cold calls / by Michael D. Krause.
        p. cm.
(alk. paper)
1. Selling. 2. Sales personnel. I. Title.
    HF5438.25.K73 2013
    658.85—dc23   2012038430

After many years of struggle and getting my PhD from the School of Hard Knocks, it is a great honor to present to you *Smart Prospecting That Works Every Time!*

I want to dedicate this solution to *you*—the person in search of sales greatness and sales success.

I have devoted my life to selling, and it's my relentless passion to help you not struggle as much as I have in my sales career. I want to inspire you to sell more than you ever imagined and show you how to be successful in selling. I want you to have the luxuries in life that you and your family deserve.

What you are about to learn will completely change your life forever. It will make "sales sense" to you, and a lightbulb will go off in your mind. You will achieve new heights that you thought were only for the chosen few.

Follow this step-by-step process and you will achieve sales success.

To Your Sales Success!

Mike

CONTENTS

ACKNOWLEDGMENTS

Writing this book has been more than a four-year journey and one of my lifelong dreams to accomplish. I'm thankful to have a wonderful family and friends who allow me to be me and be my creative self. I'm grateful to my clients who allow me to beta test my theories and ideas out in the field with them.

To Cheryl Freer, my assistant and friend, for helping make sense of my ideas and make them easy to understand to the reader, I'm forever grateful.

To my agent, Leticia Gomez at Savvy Literary Services, for believing in me and helping me navigate through the complexities of becoming a published author.

To the amazing and dynamic team at McGraw-Hill for publishing this book and making it the best of the best.

I truly have loved this journey, and I'm grateful to be surrounded by extremely talented people who help me be the best I can be.

INTRODUCTION

◆◆◆

Sales (common) sense is not so common.

What if you could see more qualified people every day in every business week? How would that affect your sales income? Statistically, it should improve your sales effectiveness and bring in more money for you.

Seven to ten days. That's the average amount of time it should take you to set up an appointment to see the decision maker at a well-researched targeted company.

Arguably the most important step in any sales cycle is setting up a first appointment with a prospective client. There is so much that must be done correctly before you are finally granted the opportunity to sit down with that prospect and help him understand how you can help him do business better, more efficiently, or more cost-effectively. Remember, you get only one chance to make that all-important first impression.

Here are some compelling sales facts for you to consider:

1. A lead that is called five minutes after it was generated is 22 times more likely to close than one called after 30 minutes.
2. Seventy-eight percent of prospects who convert to a sale do so with the company that first called them.
3. The average lead takes between five and nine attempts to reach.
4. Those who make changes in their sales process regularly achieve over 40 percent improvement in close rates.

5. Forty percent of Internet leads convert eventually *if* they are consistently followed up.

A Culpepper and Associates compensation survey and services study on the sales industry discovered the following:

- 94% of all sales veterans have had fewer than five days of formal sales training.
- 87% of all sales managers have had fewer than eight days of formal sales training.
- 98% of all salespeople don't follow a consistent sales method.
- 93% of all salespeople volunteer a price decrease without being asked.
- 87% of prospect inquiries are never followed up by a sales contact.
- 81% of all sales take five calls or more.
- 80% of all salespeople are willing to accept a 90 percent rejection rate.
- 40% of all sales veterans experience bouts of call reluctance severe enough to threaten their contribution in sales.
- 93% of all sales veterans have had no training in how to generate their own leads.

So where does *Smart Prospecting That Works Every Time!* fit in? It's the next generation of selling by leveraging modern-day technology with old-school proven sales tactics. We have all heard that Web 2.0, with its widespread information sharing, interoperability, collaboration, and user-centered design, is quickly being upstaged by Web 3.0, with its sophisticated and complex applications, greater device independence, portability, and even greater processing power.

Similarly, harnessing new technology innovations catapults the professional salesperson into a selling universe. SMART Prospecting provides you with a fresh take on the traditional sales appointment–setting guidelines, along with a briefcase full of advanced tools and applications. This lets you speed and simplify the SMART Prospecting process: from identifying your prospect right through the all-important first face-to-face meeting.

I like using SMART as an acronym for thorough, successful prospecting. It lets you as a professional salesperson really zero in on the prospect to succeed in selling beyond your wildest dreams:

S: solutions. Solve your clients' problems.
M: measure. Measure your success.
A: attitude. Stay positive.
R: resilience. Know how to handle objections.
T: trusted advisor. Be an invaluable resource to your clients.

Whether you are a single-person business, a new sales professional in a small company, or the sales manager in a Fortune 500 multinational corporation, getting a first appointment with a prospect is a universal challenge. True, some of the preliminary work may have been done for you with automated searches, but in every instance, you'll have to take virtually the same steps to find prospects and set appointments that lead to a successful sale.

Although we'll be referring to "you" throughout this book, meaning you the individual salesperson, it could mean you the corporation or business entity just as easily. Don't go into this thinking that it may not apply because you're part of a larger entity or a one-person enterprise. Efficient SMART Prospecting is an invaluable skill that not many professional salespeople master without years of trial and error, much to the detriment of their income year after year.

This book provides you with the updated fundamental steps that lead to setting up that first appointment so that you can consistently be successful.

It's our natural inclination as human beings to just *do* something—anything. But in this instance, what you must do first is research, learn, and experiment—and then probably change your process. Yes, we'll be going back to square one and starting the whole prospecting process anew; when something isn't working, that's the time to get back to basics and figure out what went wrong along the way.

When you have mastered and internalized these steps, it will be time to make that first call.

HOW TO USE THIS BOOK

This is a journal for your success: a road map and a learning tool for you to discover your unique sales style. I want to warn you that this is not a quick-fix overnight miracle pill, and I would never sell you any dream that could not be fulfilled. It is critical that you follow my proven step-by-step process to maximize your earnings potential—starting right now.

Do you think success is easy? Guess again. It is only through focus and diligence that true success is achieved. I believe in you, and I want you to be a lifelong friend and client of mine. The question is, Do you believe in yourself? I know life can be challenging, especially in this new age of a leaderless society. I mean this in a good way, because I want to inspire you to reach new heights. I will pave the runway and give you the plane; *you* have to supply the fuel. You can do this!

Just read each page and study it over and over. How many times do you think an Olympic athlete practices the same move? One time? Two or three times? Try in the thousands to get it right. Experts generally agree that it takes about 10,000 hours for someone to become accomplished at a specific skill. Succeeding in sales is no different. To be in the top 10 percent, you have to practice, practice, and then practice some more. There are no shortcuts. Put in the work, and the work will pay off tenfold.

◆◆◆

Every profession requires practice. Why do you think you're any different just because you're in sales? Practice what you learn every day.

Do the following as you go through the book:

Read the section, apply the principle, tweak, read again and apply the principle, tweak over and over until you have it down cold.

After going through this cycle a few times, you will be much better equipped to make appointment-setting calls in the business world.

Above all, remember that you must sell to people in the way they want to be sold to. Follow *their buying* process, not *your selling* process. Without a doubt, one of the biggest mistakes I see is the sales professional losing control over the sales process. Once that happens, trust me, it's all over.

At the end of each sales call, ask yourself: What's the next step?

Have you clearly identified the four critical elements to move the sales process forward? The four elements to move any sales forward are the following:

1. *Pain points.* Have you asked enough of the correct questions to understand the prospect's needs and find his true pain points?
2. *Time frame.* Have you asked about when she would like the service or product to be completed?
3. *Decision maker.* Do you have the true decision maker or just the person who thinks he is?
4. *Budget.* Have you asked about the resources that will pay for the services or products?

If you don't have answers to these questions, you are *not* in control of your selling process. When you practice your sales skills over and over, knowing what the next step is will become automatic. The question I always ask my private clients is "What's the next step?" until they're so sick of hearing it that they start any response with "The next step is . . ."

Smart Prospecting
That Works Every Time!

CHAPTER 1

◆ ◆ ◆

HOW DOES A PROSPECT THINK?

*The value of identity, of course, is that so often
with it comes purpose.*

RICHARD GRANT

THE STORY OF PAT

When I was a financial advisor, I was promoted very quickly to territory manager. While in that position, I met Pat (not his real name). Pat had been laid off by an engineering firm and had decided to become a financial advisor.

Pat was a sweetheart and very analytical, just as one would expect an engineer to be. He took meticulous notes and rounded to the tenth of a cent on his financial plans. On the surface, he and the job seemed to be a great fit. However, over time, it became apparent that Pat could not get out of his own way and perform the steps needed to succeed in selling.

I tried and he tried for months, and frankly, it was painful for Pat, his clients, and me. No one wanted Pat to fail. Especially me.

Long story short: Pat was very C with very little D, I, or S. (You will learn in a minute what this means.) He was a *get it right* person and prided himself on his ability to analyze. However, he could communicate effectively only with other C people, and that limited him in his sales and approach.

He would come into an appointment with a mountain of paper before each meeting, armed with every word, note, slide, and chart he could assemble. Sadly, there are only a few people who liked and appreciated all his data—and who were able to comprehend it. By the end of the appointment, he had scared most clients off by making his process appear too complex and too numbers-driven.

Pat was an engineer through and through. He was *not* a sales professional. He could not adapt his selling process to each prospect and navigate through the process by which the prospect needed to be sold and serviced.

I remember clearly the moment when we sat down in his office and I asked him the following question:

"Pat, how do you like sales?" (I deliberately omitted the words *financial advisor* from our conversation because financial advising was and still is a sales career.)

"Mike, I don't think sales is for me. I'm more of an engineer."

"I agree, Pat."

There are two morals to the story of Pat:

1. Sales is not for everyone.
2. You must always adapt to your client's style, not expect them to adapt to your style.

◆◆◆

Most salespeople look at sales as "just a job," not as a career.
Selling is the best career in the world. Make it your career
and you will improve your successes immeasurably.

SALESPERSON DEFINITIONS

Let's get started with some important definitions:

Sales clown. A sales representative often has poor follow-up, dresses like a slob, cares about himself or herself more than the client, is commission-driven in a bad way, uses poor English, always looks for the easy way out, is focused on the negative, works a strict nine-to-five schedule, makes excuses rather than sales, has no written goals, and lacks a well-considered sales process.

Sales professional. Anyone can be a sales professional. It takes more effort to be a sales professional, but it is definitely worth the extra work. Sales professionals think about solving the client's problems in the most clear and efficient way possible. They are always on. Their responses are quick and to the point. Sales professionals are not BS artists. They practice their messages regularly to master their craft and then communicate in a clear and concise manner. They work to make sure they never sell the wrong product to the wrong prospect. They are focused on the long-term relationship, stay positive, and are always value-driven. They are nurturers.

◆◆◆

If you say you'll do it, make sure you do it.

KNOW THYSELF

Before you can begin connecting with prospects successfully, you need to spend a bit of time and introspection figuring out who you are, who they are, and what approaches and techniques will work best for you and for them. After all, the entire objective of a sales process is to create a win-win situation for you and your customers. Before you can get started, you have to know who the players are: the people you will be contacting and yourself.

"Know thyself" was Socrates's guiding principle. There has been no better advice in the history of humanity. As Dr. Anna Spencer of the Infinity Institute observes, knowing thyself "makes unhappiness, fear, sadness, doubt, and all the negative emotions meaningless."[1]

Without a firm command of your personality style *and* a solid assessment of your prospect's personality style and learning style, your prospecting process and sales cycle have a poor chance of success. In other words, you're gambling with your income.

◆◆◆

Understand your prospect before you try to make him or her understand you.

DiSC BEHAVIOR ASSESSMENT

There are a number of popular psychological and personality inventories that help people discover their particular behavior styles. One of the most popular is the DiSC assessment, which was developed by John Geier and was based on the 1928 work of the psychologist William Moulton Marston, the behaviorist Walter V. Clarke, and others. The DiSC Assessment is owned and managed by Inscape Publishing, which commercialized the assessment and transformed it from a textbook theory to a workplace tool more than 30 years ago.

The DiSC assessment looks at how individuals act in their accustomed environment or in a specific situation such as a sales call.

There are a number of benefits from using the DiSC profile to better understand your actions and behaviors and those of your prospects, including the following:

- Discovering your behavioral strengths
- Learning to value the strengths of others
- Discovering ways to deal with conflict effectively
- Cultivating teamwork and reducing team conflict
- Developing strategies to meet diverse needs
- Improving communication skills by determining communication styles
- Increasing sales skills by understanding client or customer behaviors and decision-making styles

- Improving customer relationships and customer satisfaction
- Reducing personal and organizational conflict and stress
- Enhancing and developing coaching and mentoring skills[2]

THE DiSC LEARNING MODEL

The DiSC Profile is a nonjudgmental objective tool for understanding behavior types and personality styles. It helps people explore their behavior and the behavior of others across four primary dimensions. The Everything DiSC® Sales Profile is just one of the specialized profiles produced by Inscape Publishing to assist professionals in connecting more effectively with their customers.[3]

Dominance. Ds are direct, to the point, and decisive. As customers, Ds have a strong drive to get immediate results and accomplish their goals quickly. Their focus on the bottom line and decisiveness may appear intense and even blunt. They tend to be strong-minded and strong-willed, and they enjoy challenges, taking action, and immediate results. In working with D people, get to the point quickly, summarize rather than explain, keep questions to a minimum, and exhibit your best "can-do" attitude.

People with low D scores want to do more research before committing to a decision. They are typically conservative, low-key, cautious, cooperative, undemanding, cautious, mild-mannered, and agreeable. Here's where your lengthy explanations and myriad questions are appropriate and appreciated.

Influence. Is tend to be optimistic, outgoing, accepting, and warm. They are social people who prefer being on teams, sharing ideas, entertaining, and energizing others. I customers tend to see the sales process as another opportunity to socialize and establish a personal relationship with their salesperson. Customers with high I ranking often enjoy or start off-topic conversations that encourage a friendly, informal atmosphere.

Low I scorers are more convinced by facts and data, not with feelings and hunches. They are factual, reflective, skeptical, matter-of-fact, critical, suspicious, logical, and more pessimistic. Stick to the facts, data, and basics with low I prospects.

Steadiness. Ss are empathetic, cooperative, accepting, and warm yet cautious and reflective. They tend to be supportive, helpful team players and are often good listeners. While S customers are self-deprecating and soft-spoken, they also tend to be careful or reluctant decision makers. They prefer being in the background, working in consistent and predictable ways. They also tend to be uncomfortable with change. You will want to make sure your S customers have all the facts and figures at hand to make their decisions.

Low S scores are found in people who like change and variety. These people could be described as restless, impatient, impulsive, demonstrative, or eager. The S buying style is the polar opposite of the D buying style.

Conscientiousness. Cs tend to be concerned with details. They are reflective, questioning, and often skeptical. They focus on quality over other values. They plan ahead, check for accuracy, and act systematically. Even if they like what you are selling, they may not display much enthusiasm or animation. Stick to the facts and avoid small talk or personal anecdotes with Cs. C buying-style customers are in stark contrast with I style customers.

As you read these brief descriptions, you probably recognized a couple of your own traits in each of them. That occurred because nearly every person is a composite of the four behavior styles. But you will probably find that one or two of the styles dictate more of your actions and tendencies than the others.

Similarly, your prospects and customers will be some combination of the four behavior styles as well. In your first interactions with a new prospect, develop some casual questions of your own to help determine where they fit on the DiSC circle. This will pay dividends throughout your sales process by helping you to keep the sale moving forward at a reasonable pace.

If you are interested in taking the DiSC Profile online, go to http://www.discprofile.com/products.htm.

CONNECT-CONNECT-CONNECT

Always remember to make a connection in every personal interaction with your prospect or client, whether it be name-dropping, sharing information, connecting on social media, relating a brief story, or sending a personal item to that prospect or client. It's the little things that add up BIG! I always send a handwritten thank-you note to every person I meet in the sales process to start to grow the relationship. I sent a note to a gatekeeper once, and you would have thought I donated a kidney to her. For months my name was in the lobby where she sat, and my card was in view so everyone in the building, including competitors, knew that Michael Krause sent her a handwritten note.

Every client and prospect I meet receives an invitation to connect with me on LinkedIn. I always look as well for a newsletter to sign up for, Twitter account to follow them, YouTube channel to subscribe to, I want them to know that I care and I want to grow the relationship with them and be here for years to come.

Bottom line: You, as a sales professional, need to connect the dots throughout the maze of selling. Even if you're not, guess who is actively working the selling maze? Your competitors.

"Your competitors have virtually the same solution as you. It's YOU the prospect is buying!"

WORKING WITH PERSONAL BEHAVIOR STYLES

The chart on the next page[4] shows you the top-level behaviors from each of the quadrants of the assessment. As we work through the later chapters in this book and SMART Prospecting approaches, we'll return to this model to find ways to adapt your voice mails, e-mails, and telephone scripts to each behavioral style.

	D Direct/ Decisive *Get It Done*	**I** Interested/ Lively *Get Appreciated*	**S** Accommodating *Get Along*	**C** Precise/ Reflective *Get It Right*
Major goals	• Results • Control • Take charge	• People involvement • Recognition	• Security • Stability	• Accuracy • Order • Perfection
Major fears	• Losing control • Being taken advantage of	• Rejection • Loss of approval	• Sudden change • Losing security	• Criticism of performance • Lack of standards
Dislikes	• Being controlled by others • Lack of results	• Handling complex details • Working alone	• Hostility • Unpredictability	• Disorganization
Under pressure	• Domineering • Impatient • Rude	• Emotional • Disorganized	• Conforming • Indecisive	• Withdrawing • Stubborn
Responds to	• Options • Efficiency • Control	• Testimonials • Saving personal effort	• Assurance of stability • Personal attention	• Evidence of quality • Logical approaches
Decision style	• Quick	• Gut feel	• Deliberate	• Analytical

How to Interact, Persuade, and Sell Effectively with Each Quadrant

Here is some advice on ways to deal with people who fall into these quadrants:

D: *Get It Done*

- Be clear, specific, brief, and to the point.
- Stick to business.
- Focus on the logic and practicality of ideas and approaches.
- Present the facts concisely.

- Ask specific—preferably "what"—questions; avoid "and" questions.
- Talk about the probability of success or the effectiveness of options.
- Agree or disagree with the facts and results, not with the person.
- After talking business, depart graciously.
- Don't ramble, waste time, or ask useless questions.
- Don't try to build a personal relationship.
- Don't direct or order.
- Don't leave loopholes or cloudy issues.
- Don't come with a ready-made decision and try to get the prospect to agree.
- Don't offer multiple alternatives. Focus on the best idea that gets results.
- Don't speculate wildly or offer guarantees and assurances when there is a risk in meeting them.
- If you disagree, don't let it reflect on the prospect personally.
- If you agree, don't reinforce it by saying, "I'm with you."

I: Get Appreciated

- Plan interactions that support their dreams.
- Leave time for socializing.
- Talk about people, their goals, and topics they find stimulating.
- Put details in writing or structure the task for your prospects.
- Ask for their opinions and ideas about people.
- Provide ideas for implementing action.
- Plan for enough time to be stimulating, fun-loving, and fast-moving.
- Provide testimonials from people they see as important.
- Offer special, immediate, and extra incentives for their willingness to take risks.
- Focus on the positive consequences their actions will have for others.
- Don't legislate.

- Don't be cold or unfeeling.
- Don't focus on facts and figures, alternatives, and theories.
- Don't leave decisions hanging in the air.
- Don't try to be task-oriented.
- Don't dream with them.
- Don't stick too closely to the agenda.
- Don't talk down to them.
- Don't be dogmatic.

S: *Get Along*

- Start with a personal comment. Break the ice slowly.
- Show sincere interest in your prospect as a person. Find an area of common involvement.
- Patiently draw out personal goals and work with your prospects to help them achieve those goals.
- Listen and be responsive.
- Present your case softly in a nonthreatening manner.
- Present ideas in an organized manner by listing specific steps and items in sequence.
- Ask "how" questions to draw out their opinions.
- Watch carefully for possible areas of early disagreement or dissatisfaction.
- Act in a casual, informal manner.
- Show that their decisions will minimize risks.
- Give assurances that you will provide them with benefits.
- Provide personal assurances and specific solutions with maximum guarantees.
- Don't make promises you can't keep.
- Don't rush headlong into business or the agenda.
- Don't stick coldly to business.
- Don't lose sight of goals.
- Don't force them to respond quickly to your objections.
- Don't be domineering or demanding.
- Don't debate about facts and figures.

- Don't manipulate or bully them into agreeing even though they probably won't fight back.
- Don't be abrupt or rapid.

C: *Get It Right*

- Prepare your case in advance.
- Stick to business.
- Approach them in a straightforward, direct way.
- Support their principles by using a thoughtful approach.
- Build your credibility by listing pros and cons for any suggestion you make.
- Make an organized contribution to their efforts.
- Present specifics.
- Do what you say you will do.
- Take your time but be persistent.
- Draw up a scheduled approach to implementing action with a step-by-step timetable.
- Assure them that there won't be surprises.
- Give them time to verify the reliability of your actions.
- Be accurate and realistic.
- Provide solid, tangible, practical evidence.
- Don't use the testimonials of others, particularly those of unreliable sources.
- When appropriate, give them time to be thorough.
- Provide exact descriptions of expectations and plans and show how they fit into the overall plan.
- Don't be disorganized or messy.
- Don't be casual, informal, or loud.
- Don't ramble, act in a disorganized way, or leave things to chance or luck.
- Don't rush the decision-making process.
- Don't push too hard or be unrealistic with deadlines.
- Don't be vague about what's expected of either of you.
- Don't fail to follow through.

Now Behave

1. Based on the descriptions and the chart on the foregoing pages, make an educated guess about your most prominent behavior style in the following chart. Appendix A lets you make an assessment of the shared traits and behaviors you have with your prospects. Pay close attention to what you share and to where your traits and behaviors diverge.

Your Behavior Style

Symbol	Total	Dominant Behavior
D		Get it done
I		Get appreciated
S		Get along
C		Get it right

2. For one of your current sales prospects, make your best assessment of his or her behavior style on the basis of what you have been able to learn about the person from public sources or personal association. Total the results here.

Prospect Behavior Style

Symbol	Total	Dominant Behavior
D		Get it done
I		Get appreciated
S		Get along
C		Get it right

3. On the basis of the chart and the interaction recommendations on the previous pages, how should you approach this decision maker?

KOLB'S EXPERIENTIAL LEARNING STYLES MODEL

With a better command of your own learning style and by applying those insights to your prospects, you will have greater success in selling. The information about people's behavior explained in the previous section, coupled with the descriptions of learning styles we'll cover below, will provide you with the formula you need to approach anyone and achieve professional rapport, allowing you to earn more money. You will sell to anyone without feeling frustrated and will avoid the fatal error of failing at a sale because of a personality clash. Until I started adopting these strategies in my selling, I often found myself on the wrong end of a lost sale and without a clue as to why I hadn't succeeded.

◆ ◆ ◆

Finding commonality is the first step in relationship selling.

Knowing more about the personality and learning dimensions of your prospects and yourself is invaluable and will keep you from following too closely on my (then clueless) heels.

Having developed the model over many years, David Kolb published his learning styles model in 1984. The model gave rise to terms such as *experiential learning theory* (ELT) and *learning styles inventory* (LSI). In his publications, notably his 1984 book *Experiential Learning: Experience as the Source of Learning and Development*, Kolb acknowledges the early work on experiential learning by some great minds of the earlier 1900s, including Carl Rogers, Carl Gustav Jung, and Jean Piaget.

Kolb's learning theory sets out four distinct learning styles based on a four-stage learning cycle. Kolb's model offers both a way to understand individual people's learning styles and an explanation of the cycle of experiential learning that applies to us all.

Kolb includes this cycle of learning as a central principle in his experiential learning theory. In his four-stage cycle of learning, immediate or concrete experiences provide a basis for observations and reflections.

Kolb says that ideally, though not always, a learner touches all the bases, that is, goes through a spiral or cycle of experiencing, reflecting, thinking, and acting. Immediate or concrete experiences lead to observations and reflections. Those reflections are assimilated (absorbed and translated) into abstract concepts with implications for action that the person can actively test and experiment with and that then enable the creation of new experiences.

Kolb's model works on two levels of a four-stage learning cycle:

1. Concrete experience (CE)
2. Reflective observation (RO)
3. Abstract conceptualization (AC)
4. Active experimentation (AE)

Kolb includes a four-type definition of learning styles, each representing the combination of two steps in the cycle, rather like a two-by-two matrix of the four-stage cycle:

1. Diverging (CE/RO)
2. Assimilating (AC/RO)
3. Converging (AC/AE)
4. Accommodating (CE/AE)

Kolb explains that different people naturally prefer a certain single learning style. Various factors influence a person's preferred style: in his experiential learning theory model (ELT), Kolb defines three stages of a person's development and suggests that people's propensity to reconcile and successfully integrate the four different learning styles improves as they mature through the development stages.

The development stages that Kolb identified are as follows:

1. *Acquisition:* birth to adolescence; the development of basic abilities and cognitive structures
2. *Specialization:* schooling, early work, and personal experiences of adulthood; the development of a particular specialized learning style shaped by social, educational, and organizational socialization
3. *Integration:* midcareer through to later life; the expression of nondominant learning styles in work and personal life

Whatever influences a person's choice of style, the learning style preference is actually the product of two pairs of variables, or two separate choices that people make, which Kolb presented as lines of axis, each with conflicting or oppositional modes at either end.

These lines of axis correspond to Kolb's two continua. The horizontal axis is the processing continuum—the way people approach a task—and the vertical axis is the perception continuum—people's emotional response, or the way they think or feel about it.

Kolb's research proved that people cannot do—watch and think—and feel (experience both the processing and the perception continua) at the same time. When we experience a learning situation in which we want to do both, it creates conflict internally that is ultimately resolved by an unconscious choice. Each person subconsciously decides whether to do or watch and at the same time whether to think or feel.

The result of these two decisions produces and helps form the preferred learning style individuals will use throughout their lives, as shown in the two-by-two matrix below. We choose a way of grasping an experience that defines our approach to it. We also choose a way to transform that experience into something meaningful and usable that defines our emotional response to the experience.

Therefore, every person's learning style is a product of these two choice decisions:

1. How we approach a task—that is, *grasp an experience*—preferring to:
   a. Watch
   b. Do
2. Our emotional response to the experience—that is, *transform the experience*—preferring to:
   a. Think
   b. Feel

It's easy to visualize the construction of Kolb's learning styles in a two-by-two matrix. The diagram also highlights Kolb's terminology for the four learning styles: diverging, assimilating, converging, and accommodating.

	Doing Active experimentation (AE)	**Watching** Reflective observation (RO)
Feeling Concrete experience (CE)	Accommodating (CE/AE)	Diverging (CE/RO)
Thinking Abstract conceptualization (AC)	Converging (AC/AE)	Assimilating (AC/RO)

For example, a person with a dominant learning style of doing rather than watching the task and feeling rather than thinking about the experience will learn best when the learning experience combines those processes; this is the accommodating learning style in Kolb's terminology.

This brief description of the four Kolb learning styles gives you a general profile of how people with these learning styles may behave:

- *Diverging (feeling and watching; CE/RO).* These people are able to look at concrete situations from multiple perspectives. They are sensitive. They prefer to watch rather than do, tending to gather information and then use their imagination to solve the problem. Kolb called this style diverging because these people perform better in situations that require idea generation, for example, brainstorming. People with a diverging learning style have broad cultural interests. They are interested in people, tend to be imaginative and emotional, and tend to be strong in the arts. They listen with an open mind, prefer to work in groups, and want to receive personal feedback.
- *Assimilating (watching and thinking; AC/RO).* The assimilating learning preference involves a concise, logical approach. These people require a good clear explanation rather than a practical opportunity. They excel at understanding wide-ranging information and organizing it into a clear and logical format. People with an assimilating learning style are less focused on people and more interested in ideas and abstract concepts. People with this style are more attracted to logically sound

theories than to approaches based on practical value. This learning style is quite effective for people in information and science careers. In formal learning situations, people with this style prefer reading, attending lectures, exploring analytical models, and having time to think things through.

- *Converging (doing and thinking; AC/AE)*. People with a converging learning style can solve problems and will use their learning to find solutions to practical issues. People with a converging learning style are best at finding practical uses for ideas and theories. These people are more attracted to technical tasks and problems than to social or interpersonal issues. A converging learning style is particularly useful for specialists and people who work with technology. People with this style like to experiment with new ideas, simulate, and work with practical applications.
- *Accommodating (doing and feeling; CE/AE)*. The accommodating learning style is hands-on and relies on intuition and gut instinct rather than logical analysis. These people rely on other people's information and analysis and prefer to take a practical, experiential approach. They are attracted to new challenges and experiences and to carrying out plans. This learning style is prevalent and useful in roles requiring action and initiative. People with an accommodating learning style prefer to work in teams to complete tasks. They set targets and actively work in the field, trying different ways to achieve an objective.

Knowing these four styles can make a significant difference in your method of connecting with a prospect. Imagine that you have an accommodating style and are approaching a person with an assimilating style. How well will it work if you insist that that person take the controls and operate the product or browse within a user interface on his or her computer? Some people jump at that chance, such as a fellow Accommodating. But a good many people—a Diverging, for instance—would be far more comfortable watching you and getting the hang of it that way.

Of course, no one you'll encounter is this basic and clear cut. Each person's schooling and previous experiences will result in a blend of these styles, and so you are not likely to be able to label yourself or anyone else as a pure Accommodating or a pure Converging.

Further, it isn't life or death if you don't exactly know your prospect's learning style, though this certainly can be a useful tool when you do demonstrations, create presentations, or explain how a process, service, or product operates. You need to be able to frame your words, actions, and explanations differently so that people with different styles of learning are able to comprehend what you are selling.

◆◆◆

Showing versus telling is the path to sales success.

FOUR LEARNING STYLES

Another classic approach to learning involves the following four types of learning styles:

- *Spatial and visual*: employs graphics, diagrams, and presentations that cement the lesson or information
- *Tactile and kinetic*: integrates physical movement and activity into the learning process
- *Auditory*: learns best by hearing the information, such as through verbal presentations, lectures, and audio CDs
- *Logical*: needs to analyze information; problem solving, abstract questioning, repeating back what they have heard[4]

Most people don't fit precisely into any of these four styles of learning and are a combination of auditory with spatial and visual, learning best by seeing and hearing the information at the same time. The best idea is to integrate all four types of learning modes as much as possible into your sales approach to make sure you are connecting effectively with your target audience regardless of their learning styles.

Master Behavior and Learning Styles

Try this approach with one of your sales prospects:

1. Referring to Kolb's learning behaviors, describe your personal learning style. Remember that you probably have a combination of styles.
2. For one of your current sales prospects, ideally the same person for whom you assessed behavior styles in the earlier exercise, use whatever information or clues you have to formulate an opinion about that person's learning style.
3. Using what you have learned from the discussions of behavior and learning style in this chapter, identify shared and unique traits for you and your prospect that you should keep in mind in approaching this prospect.

Use the Prospect Psychology Template in Appendix B.

Here is a little something extra to think about. Answer these questions for yourself:

- My clients like me because . . .
- If I left the business today, my clients/prospects/coworkers would miss . . .
- I love being in sales because . . .
- Would I buy from me?

FEAR OF REJECTION

◆◆◆

No is just the beginning.

From an early age, nearly every person has developed some fear of rejection by playmates, dates, teachers, and parents. Most people successfully resolve these feelings of rejection by the time they are in their early twenties. According to psychologists, the best cure is to understand better who you are and develop strong self-esteem and a healthy self-image.

However, with the sales profession requiring sales professionals to put themselves out there and risk rejection every day, a majority of salespeople still have some concerns about rejection. These concerns aren't necessarily obvious or consciously acknowledged to themselves personally or to anyone around them. Any one or several of the following statements may indirectly express a salesperson's fear of rejection:

- I don't want to appear to be too pushy.
- I'm afraid they'll say no.
- I don't want to pick up the phone.
- I misplaced his business card, and so it will be a hassle to track him down.
- I've got a lot of paperwork to catch up on this week; maybe next week will be better.
- I don't know how she will receive me.
- If they want my products or services, they know how to contact me.
- I don't know what to say.
- I'm not sure how they're going to remember me.
- I keep meaning to call him but just never get around to it.
- I don't think she wants or can afford our product or service.
- I heard something negative about his company (or him), so I'm not going to call.
- I'm just too busy right now with other things.
- I don't think I'll get anything out of calling her.
- Turns out I can't deliver what I told him I could.

Do any of these statements sound familiar? We've all said or thought them at one time or another. The best defense against this mindset is a great offense. My personal approach is to think briefly about what would be the worst thing that could possibly happen and then telephone or visit the prospect in the office anyway.

The very worst outcome is that somewhere within the sales process, your top prospect decides that he or she doesn't want your service or product. Does this mean that you have been rejected? No! *You* have not been rejected; your offer of a dynamite product or service solution has been declined. You—the person—are still whole and intact, so take it in stride and move on.

◆◆◆

Rejection is just another part of the sales process. It's not personal.

INACTIVITY IS A DECISION

Although you may fool yourself (and others) with some of the reasons or excuses listed on page 20, your reluctance to make the sales calls for which you are responsible is ultimately your own decision, and you create your own future of successful or unsuccessful selling.

When you catch yourself deciding not to make those calls, think about how it appears to your prospect when you do not call as expected:

- Your prospect gave you clear permission and approval to contact her.
- Your prospect is expecting (maybe even looking forward to) your call.
- You committed to calling the prospect on a particular day and time.
- Not calling is a breach of personal trust and business etiquette.
- You are simply continuing the conversation you were having last week.
- You actually met this prospect recently in person.
- You came away from your introduction to the prospect with the distinct impression that his company is a qualified lead and that this prospect does have a sincere need or interest in your products or services.

- You believe that your products or services will improve the prospect's company's operations or business.
- You can easily demonstrate your benefits to her business.
- You can support your benefits with testimonials and case studies.
- There's potential for additional business once the relationship is initiated.

◆◆◆

Cold = gold.

WHAT IF YOU DON'T . . .

. . . make the call? If you promised to call someone after a networking event, a trade show, an impromptu conversation at the coffee shop, or a shared cab ride to the airport and you don't call when you said you would, here is a quick list of the consequences you face:

1. You tarnish your reputation within the business community. That alone is bad for your long-term success in the business world. In addition, you are your company's representative, and so you also damage your company's reputation. That's a big deal too. Your company is judged on the behavior you exhibit in your dealings with the prospect. If you are unprofessional, unreliable, or untrustworthy, the entire company can be written off in a matter of minutes through your personal fault. You must take seriously your responsibility to act professionally and as an ambassador for your company in all your on-the-job and leisure activities.
2. The prospect assumes that you don't care about his business and thinks (or says), "Well, that sure was a waste of time."
3. You are judged to be unreliable or even a liar, and your integrity is severely jeopardized. Your prospect will think, Hey, if she can't be counted on at this early stage of our business relation-

ship, how will I be treated (and my company be treated) if I do become her client?

4. You are not to be trusted or believed. You broke your promise by not calling as you said you would. How can the prospect believe what you will say down the road?

5. Rather than making the first move and risking rejection, you are rejecting the prospect. This is not the way to make a success of selling.

6. Without putting yourself out there, you will never know how you and your company might have benefited from this prospect and from the prospect's future business referrals.

7. Betraying this new prospect's trust in this way is worse than never having made his acquaintance in the first place.

8. By disrespecting this prospect's interest in your product and services, you risk generating waves of negativity and a poor customer-relations reputation for your company. You know that the prospect is very likely to tell others within her company or even at other businesses.

9. When you run into this prospect at another function, how will you feel, and how are you going to handle your embarrassment?

CONTROL THAT FEAR

◆ ◆ ◆
Do not fear cold calling: every relationship starts out cold.

No one likes to hear the word *no*. However, an unequivocal no is the second best answer you will ever get. Not knowing where you stand with a prospect is the worst position to be in.

◆ ◆ ◆
Sell and live by this motto: Every floor and every door.

CONNECT-CONNECT-CONNECT

Always remember to make a connection in every personal interaction with your prospect or client whether it be name-dropping, sharing information, connecting on social media, relating a brief story, or sending a personal item to that person. It's the little things that add up big! I always send a handwritten thank-you note to every person I meet in the sales process because this helps start the relationship. I sent a note to a gatekeeper once, and you would have thought I donated a kidney to her. For months my name was in the lobby where she sat and my card was in view so that everyone in the building, including competitors, knew that Michael D. Krause had sent her a handwritten note.

Every client and prospect I meet receives an invitation to connect with me on LinkedIn. I always look as well for a newsletter to sign up for, Twitter account to follow, and YouTube channel to subscribe to. I want them to know that I care, and I want to grow the relationship with them and be there for years to come.

Bottom line: When I'm consulting with my clients and I'm out on sales calls with them, the prospect will invariably say, "I thought I was too small for your company or that you just didn't like us." This happens all the time. Make those calls into accounts even though someone claimed that you would never get or that they did not like you. It's more than likely to be a misunderstanding, and they often turn out to be your best clients. You, as a sales professional, need to connect the dots throughout the maze of selling. If you're not, guess who is actively working the selling maze? Your competitor.

Your competitor has virtually the same solution as you. It's *you* the prospect is buying.

CHAPTER 2

◆ ◆ ◆

HE SHOOTS, HE SCORES!

A goal is a dream with a deadline.

NAPOLEON HILL

◆ ◆ ◆

Sales is a contact sport: the more people you contact, the more
money you will make.

WHAT ARE GOALS?

I love goals. Goals are the true difference between success and failure. The number one reason goals are not achieved is that people do
not write them down. The second reason is that the person quits and
never follows through on them.

Years ago, I discovered that I was achieving my goals every time
I wrote them down. For example, I graduated from St. Bonaventure
in 1996 with a bachelor of business administration (BBA) degree. My
goal was to show the world, go out and crush it! A lot of my classmates
stated at the time that earning $40,000 was unachievable the first year
out of college. But I didn't believe that; I didn't listen to them, and I
had my goal. At the end of my first year after college, I made $39,876,
and in my mind I had achieved what they said couldn't be done.

I reflect a lot on that goal, as it was my first real financial goal. I
often wonder what would have happened if I had not written it down

and lived it each and every day that year. I can almost guarantee that I would have made closer to $20,000—half of my original goal—and fulfilled the prophecy made by my classmates.

Some of you might say, "Mike, you didn't make $40,000 that first year; you fell short by $124! So why are you counting this as a success?" Well, because at the end of the day, a goal is a stretch, a nice "what if" that you can strive for. Then, when you almost make your stretch goal and surpass your expected target, it's even better.

By the way: your quota is only your quota, not your goal. If your sales quota is $1,000,000, your goal should be $1,200,000, or 20 percent over the quota. A quota is a minimum requirement to remain employed. Don't do the minimum. Achieving your quota will only earn you quota (that is, minimum) pay.

Since I became a consultant and started developing commission plans, I've realized that all the real money is earned when you go *over* quota. Push yourself a little every day and you can beat your quota with no problem.

Remember to break your annual quota down into daily achievable goals to achieve that year-end quota. There have been many times when I have made my goals and quota during the last week of December. I made it then because I had worked on it every day for the entire year, not just when the calendar rolled around to the last month of the year.

I remember a time when I met a client in a mall parking lot while she was doing her holiday shopping so that I could obtain her signature on an order. I made my goal by building the relationship over the previous few months and then meeting her on her time. I got her signature on the trunk of her car and then drove the order directly to FedEx. To achieve goals, you have to go that extra mile to make it happen.

Keep your goals in front of you at all times or they will be absent from your mind.

A great motivational and inspirational book you should pick up and read is *The Last Lecture* by Randy Pausch. When Pausch, a computer science professor at Carnegie Mellon, was asked to give a last lecture, he didn't have to imagine it was his last, since he had recently been diagnosed with terminal cancer. But the lecture he gave, "Really Achieving Your Childhood Dreams," wasn't about dying. It was about the importance of overcoming obstacles, of enabling the dreams of others, of seizing every moment (because "time is all you have . . . and you may find one day that you have less than you think"). It was a summation of everything Randy had come to believe. It was about *living*.

In *The Last Lecture*, Pausch combines the humor, inspiration, and intelligence that made his lecture such a phenomenon and gives it an indelible form. It is a book that will be shared for generations to come.

SETTING YOUR GOALS

According to Merriam-Webster's online dictionary, a goal (in sports) is (a) an area or object toward which players in various games attempt to advance a ball or puck and usually through or into which it must go to score points or (b) the terminal point of a race. In life, a goal is defined more vaguely: the end toward which effort is directed.

For decades, psychologists have gathered evidence about goal setting, finding that setting goals or not setting them profoundly affects individuals, companies, and even countries. Yet people tend to reject the goal-setting process as a waste of time. In the context of SMART Prospecting, you cannot achieve your goals—whether you have set them for yourself or have had them set for you by your sales manager or chief executive officer (CEO)—unless you write them down by hand (this isn't the time for computers and typing) and internalize them fully.

Zig Ziglar claims that every person chooses—consciously or unconsciously—to have no goals and accepts the consequences year after year. However, if you are serious about achieving a goal or objective (here the terms are synonymous), you must follow the goal-setting formula. Otherwise, you will never achieve your goal.

Ziglar maintains that most people are full of good intentions to do something but find myriad reasons and excuses to postpone getting started on projects or goals. He believes that most people's problem is not a lack of time to work toward their goals, as they often claim, but a lack of direction. Every one of us gets the same 24 hours a day, 7 days a week, and 365 days in a year to accomplish things. It's what we do with that time that determines whether we achieve our goals or simply continue to talk about them with great intentions.

Goals enable you to set a course for achievement and create the activities that move you toward those goals. Along the way, these structured goal-achieving activities create excitement in the progress you are making toward your goals, which in turn spurs you on to further (and quicker) achievement.

◆◆◆

Have a constant, relentless passion to achieve your goals.

SMARTER GOALS

To be effective, all goals must be:

S: *Specific.* In fact, the more specific and well defined your goals are, the better. State your goals in terms that are as precise as possible. This gives you clarity, direction, motivation, and focus. Your goal should be significant enough to inspire you to move either toward the life you want or away from something you don't want. If your goal statement is vague, you will find the goal difficult to achieve, as the definition of success will also be hard to quantify. What's your goal?

M: *Measurable.* That which you measure will be treasured, so think about how to measure the achievement of your goals. It is easier to track progress toward a goal if it is measurable. Some goals are easy to measure, such as weight loss, running speed, and income. Others are difficult to measure as there is no definable quantification for them. In these cases, you will have to create some kind of ranking system or measure the time you spend on achieving the goal. Measuring your progress helps you determine whether you are heading in the right direction so that you can make any necessary adjustments along the way to stay on course. How will you measure your goal?

A: Accountable and action-oriented. To whom or what are you accountable for your goal? What is your strategy for how you are going to achieve your goal? You don't need all the details right now; start with a general plan of action and then focus on the actions that are within your control. Are you accountable to yourself?

R: Realistic and reasoned. Unrealistic goals and time frames will lead to discouragement and abandonment of the goal. Goals should be relevant, meaningful, and significant to your life so that they will make a difference. Remind yourself why you want to achieve a particular goal. Goals should also be realistic in that the actions you need to take to achieve them are things you can actually do and control. Is your goal realistic?

T: Time-based. Decide on your timetable for completion and stick to it. For goals that have a measurable finishing point, such as weight loss, it is important (and easy) to set a deadline. Goals without deadlines lend themselves to procrastination and postponement, as in the familiar "I'll start my diet tomorrow" refrain. Individual action items leading to the goal also need deadlines to keep the momentum and motivation up. When will your goal be completed?

E: Exciting, ethical, and enjoyable. Goals have to be something you are excited about: either you are going to enjoy the process of achieving them or you will enjoy the outcome. If goals don't meet these criteria, you probably won't achieve them. Exciting goals will be reached far sooner than will boring, uninspiring goals. Are you excited about achieving your goal?

Goals also have to be ethical. Most of us are moral people with a naturally high ethical standard. Research has shown that people subconsciously resist doing things that we know or believe to be unethical. Therefore, if you set a goal with questionable ethics, subconsciously you will put off taking action on that goal. Although this might seem a silly check-off, you have to ask yourself the question so that you aren't sabotaging your goal-setting journey from the start. For the same reason, you need to be honest with yourself: your subconscious knows when you're not honest and will react by resisting your actions. Is your goal enjoyable and ethical?

R: *Recorded and resourced.* Keep a record of your goals in a place where you can see them and refer to them every day or whenever you need a reminder of why you're doing what you're doing. You also probably need to dedicate some resources toward achieving your goals. This may be time, money, external support, information, or other things. You may even have to make some sacrifices (limiting or avoiding certain foods in the weight loss example) to achieve your goals. But if your goal is truly what you want to achieve, a few personal sacrifices shouldn't deter you. No pain, no gain! How will you record progress toward your goal? Do you have the correct resources?

FEAR OF GOAL SETTING

Have you ever tried to set personal or professional goals for yourself and not succeeded? If you fail, it's likely that one of these reasons is the culprit:

1. You won't follow the process through because:
   - You just can't think of a good reason to set goals.
   - You don't see how goal setting can help you.
   - You don't have the time.

- You think it's too hard.
- You are afraid of failure or afraid you won't achieve your goals.
- You don't take it seriously enough to commit to your goals.
2. You commit one of the seven deadly sins of goal setting, which are:
   a. You don't put your goals in writing.
   b. You're unrealistic.
   c. Your motivations are unclear.
   d. You don't create a plan.
   e. You don't take action.
   f. You lose focus.
   g. Your goals and action plans aren't flexible.

Fear is natural, but it's important to remember that as humans, we've evolved to the stage where almost all of our fears are self-created. We scare ourselves out of action by imagining negative outcomes to any activities we pursue or experience. In fact, psychologists like to say that the word fear really stands for fantasized experiences appearing real.

Identify Unfounded Fears

To identify the unfounded fears in your life, complete this simple exercise. First, make a list of three things you are afraid to do. These are not things you are afraid of, such as spiders; instead, they are the things you are afraid to do, such as sky diving, making cold calls, or asking the cute server for her phone number.

Next, restate each fear in the following format:

I want to _____, and I scare myself by imagining

_____.

For example, I want to *start my own business*, and I scare myself by imagining that I *could go bankrupt and lose my house.*

I want to _____, and I scare myself by imagining

_____.

I want to _____, and I scare myself by imagining

_____.

I want to _____, and I scare myself by imagining

_____.

If we complete these statements for all the things we are afraid to do, it's easy to see how we create our own fear by imagining negative outcomes in the future.

Here are three easy techniques for moving past your fears:

1. *Dispel fear by choosing a positive mental image.* When we're afraid, our minds are full of negative thoughts and images. When you are feeling afraid, tune in to the negative images in your head. Then choose to replace them with a positive image of the desired outcome. For example, if you're afraid that starting your own business will end in bankruptcy and the loss of your house, picture instead your new business becoming wildly successful and picture yourself buying a vacation home with all the added income you're earning with your new company.

2. *Focus on the physical sensations.* You may experience fear in your body as a sinking feeling in your stomach, a tightening in your shoulders and chest, or an elevated heart rate. Focus on the feelings you'd rather be experiencing, such as peace and joy. Fix these two different impressions in your mind's eye and then move back and forth between the two, spending 15 seconds or so on each. After a minute or two, you'll find yourself feeling neutral and centered, enjoying the sensations of confidence.

3. *Recall your successes.* You've overcome countless fears to become the person you are today, whether it was learning to ride a bike, driving a car for the first time, or getting your first kiss. New experiences always feel a little scary. But when you face your

fears and jump into an experience anyway, you build confidence in your abilities. The situation you're facing now and the way your fear is manifesting may be different from what you've experienced in the past, but you know how to overcome your fears. You've spent a lifetime doing it successfully.

Feel Your Fear and Do It Anyway

Every successful person I know has been willing to take a leap of faith even though he or she was afraid. These people knew that if they didn't act, a golden opportunity would pass them by.

Recognize fear for what it is: a mental trick that your ego uses in an attempt to protect you from the negative outcomes it imagines. You create your fear, and you have the power to dissolve it. Use the techniques outlined in this section to overcome this daunting roadblock of fear so that you can turn your dreams into reality and live the life you deserve. Remember, no one achieves greatness by playing it safe.

GOAL-SETTING FORMULA

There are a number of formulas that can help you develop your personal and professional goals. The key to setting goals you will actually pay attention to is to write down *in your own writing* (not on a computer) your responses to the steps below. Then keep the answers close to you so that you can review them frequently. Writing a goal down cements it in your mind and turns it into a tangible commitment you are making to yourself rather than an aimless wish.

The steps below provide an explicit detailed process to follow:

1. Write your personal and professional or business goals down as clearly and precisely as possible. Be conservative and start with one to three goals in each category; otherwise you will burn out trying to achieve too much at one time. Consider setting at least one long-term goal and two short-term goals that work together

so that you have an immediate payback and a yardstick for measuring your achievements.

2. Date the goal on the day you write it so that you can mark the beginning of your achievement journey.

3. Identify any obstacles, risks, barriers, or issues you know of at the outset that might make it difficult to achieve your goal.

3. Name people, organizations, or companies you must work with or enlist the support of to achieve your goal.

4. Create a plan of action, including what you need to know as you begin your journey toward goal achievement.

5. Clearly describe what is in it for you as you make progress and when you achieve your goal. In other words, why do you deserve to achieve that goal?

6. Bring a positive attitude to the journey to achieving your goals. Negative self-talk will extinguish your motivation, whereas positive thoughts and expecting the best will move you past obstacles with little trouble.

7. Set a deadline for achieving your goal and, if appropriate, create a timeline of steps that will help you arrive at that goal.

8. Understand that your action plan, your time frame, or even your goal itself may need adjustment as you work through the steps. Be flexible in pursuing your goal so that you can make changes or even switch one goal for another if that makes sense in your life or your business.

9. List the benefits you will receive when you achieve your goal. If possible, use pictures or word pictures to describe how achieving your goal will feel to you—what it will look like, feel like, taste like, and so on—so that you can visualize your success and experience it with all your senses.

If it's helpful for you to see and work the goal-achieving process in the form of a graphic flowchart, review the worksheet on the following pages and work through the process boxes. If you need more space, photocopy the worksheet pages and supplement them with blank sheets of paper.

◆ ◆ ◆

Start every day with a powerful goal in front of you.

Online Goal-Setting Help

I'm sure it won't surprise you to learn that there are numerous sites online that will help you set and monitor your goals. One of the best is 43 Things (43things.com).

People have known for years that making a list of goals is the best way to achieve them, but most of us never get around to making a list. 43 Things is great for that. Make a list on 43 Things and see what changes happen in your life. Best of all, it's a way of connecting with other enthusiasts interested in everything from watching a space shuttle launch to growing one's own vegetables. The next time someone asks you, "What do you do?" you can answer with confidence, "I am doing 43 things!"

GOAL-SETTING WORKSHEET

Created by _____ for the period

_____to _____ Dated _____

Goal Setting

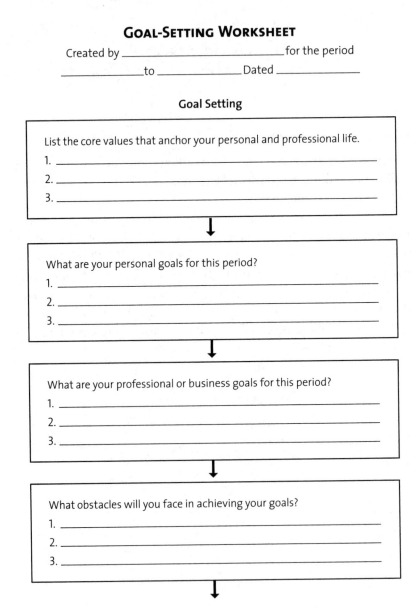

List the core values that anchor your personal and professional life.

1. _____

2. _____

3. _____

What are your personal goals for this period?

1. _____

2. _____

3. _____

What are your professional or business goals for this period?

1. _____

2. _____

3. _____

What obstacles will you face in achieving your goals?

1. _____

2. _____

3. _____

(continued top next page)

How will you overcome your obstacles?

1. _____
2. _____
3. _____

↓

What support do you need in pursuing your goals, and from whom?

1. _____
2. _____
3. _____
4. _____
5. _____

↓

What is your time frame for achieving your personal and professional goals?

Personal goal time frame _____

Professional goal time frame _____

↓

How will achievement of your goals look? Visualize every aspect of your achievement: How do you feel? What is your attitude? What are others' attitudes? Visualize and describe every detail so that realizing your goal becomes vivid and tangible to you.

1. _____
2. _____
3. _____
4. _____
5. _____
6. _____

Sales Pro Calling Success Tracker

It's critical to start each day with a specific numeric goal in front of you regarding your efforts to connect with people. You can use the following format for doing this:

Daily Sales Goals: _____ Date: _____

Dials: 100-99-98-97-96-95-94-93-92-91-90-89-88-87-86-85-84-83-82-81-80-79-78-77-76-75-74-73-72-71-70-69-68-67-66-65-64-63-62-61-60-59-58-57-56-55-54-53-52-51-50-49-48-47-46-45-44-43-42-41-40-39-38-37-36-35-34-33-32-31-30-29-28-27-26-25-24-23-22-21-20-19-18-17-16-15-14-13-12-11-10-09-08-07-06-05-04-03-02-01—Nice job!

Decision Makers: 20-19-18-17-16-15-14-13-12-11-10-09-08-07-06-05-04-03-02-01 —Great job!

Face-to-Face Appointments: 3-2-1—Unbelievable superstar!

Sales intelligence: (What did you learn about your prospects to start a conversation?)

E-mail addresses: (How many did you collect?)

20-19-18-17-16-15-14-13-12-11-10-09-08-07-06-05-04-03-02-01—Awesome Job!

Positive: (What happened that was great?)

Challenges: (What were some obstacles?)

Tweak: (What will you do differently tomorrow?)

212: The Extra Degree

You'll find a short inspirational video on YouTube.com or at www.212movie.com that was made by Simple Truths (www.simple truths.com). It uses the boiling point of water at sea level (212 degrees Fahrenheit) as an analogy for putting in just a bit more effort to achieve your goals. At 211 degrees, water is hot. At 212 degrees, water boils. That one degree of temperature (one degree of effort in life or business) makes all the difference between success and not quite enough. The point is that each person is responsible for his or her own results. All of us are accountable for everything we do or don't do in life. Turn up your personal heat just one degree and incredible things will happen for you.

The video concludes with these words:

> The only thing that stands between a person and what they want in life is the will to try it and the faith to believe it possible. Belief fuels enthusiasm. Enthusiasm explodes into passion. Passion fires our souls and lifts our spirits. Having a simple, clearly defined goal can capture the imagination and inspire passion.[1]

ACTIONS VERSUS ACCOMPLISHMENTS

Although you may be quite busy in your job or your everyday life, if you haven't identified goals or objectives toward which you are working, you are probably mistaking action and activity for accomplishment. When a task or project helps move you closer to your goals, it is an accomplishment. In an ideal scenario, you should be able to point to several accomplishments in a day, week, or month that help you on your journey toward your goal. In the context of this book, learning how to set appointments more effectively and quickly is an accomplishment that moves you closer to making more sales and thus more income:

More appointments = more closed calls = more sales = more income

Actions and activities will occupy your time, but they don't necessarily result in accomplishments. For example, if your goal is more sales through more appointments and your actions include scrolling through databases and scanning the business section of the newspaper for potential customers, these may be merely actions because they're not directly aligned with the tasks you need to perform to achieve your sales goal. Sadly, it is human nature to take the easy way out and confuse actions (also known as stall tactics or busywork) with accomplishment.

Rather than spending those ergs of energy pretending to yourself and your sales manager that you're actually accomplishing something when in reality you're just acting for the sake of acting, *do the work*. Now! There is no time like the present. Procrastinating only moves your goals farther away from you.

WHAT ABOUT THOSE RISKS, OBSTACLES, AND ISSUES?

Your prospects are conditioned to think you're lying to them. Get their concerns on the table and addressed early in the process.

If this were an ideal world, you could work through the steps outlined earlier and create your goals, then zip right along and accomplish them with no problems. However, we live in a changeable landscape that is littered with stumbling blocks from our personal lives, our professional positions, and the world at large, including economic, political, and social aspects of our lives that are beyond our control. No doubt about it, you will encounter formidable risks, obstacles, and issues as you work toward your stated goals.

Many pundits have variations on this saying, but essentially it goes like this: you can't control your environment or others' actions; all you can control is your reaction to them. Your only option when something adverse occurs is to look the challenge directly in the eye and decide what your reaction to it will be. You can adapt to the new situation and regain control by making changes to your expectations and attitude, or you can become a victim and let the situation take you down while you moan and complain.

Try the following to recast a challenge in a more objective light:

- *Reframe it.* Try to establish a more positive perspective and find the opportunity or benefit in the moment. Look for the humor in it to release your anxiety and rebalance yourself.
- *Look at the big picture.* Ask yourself how important this challenge or setback will be to you (and your goal attainment) in the long run. Will it matter in a month? Will you even remember it in a year? If the answer is no, turn your attention back to your goal achievement and move along.
- *Adjust your standards.* Don't expect perfection from yourself or others, as it simply sets you up for disappointment or failure. Set reasonable standards for yourself and others so that you don't create issues that will derail your progress.
- *Accentuate the positive.* Put your entire life in perspective by taking a few moments every day to focus on what is great in your life, including your positive qualities, talents, and drive. Then move on with your journey.

◆◆◆

Control each step in the sales process from the beginning to the end. If you're not in control, you will always be wondering what happened.

Adjusting Your Attitude

The way you think can have a profound effect on your emotional and physical well-being. Each time you think a negative thought about yourself, your body reacts as if it were in the throes of a tension-filled situation. The reverse is also true: if you see good things about yourself, you are more likely to feel good. Eliminate absolute words such as *always, never, gotta, should,* and *must* from your vocabulary and your innermost thoughts. These are the telltale marks of self-defeating thoughts.[2]

Positive thinking doesn't mean that you stick your head in the sand and ignore life's unpleasant side. It means that you approach the unpleasantness in a more positive and productive way.

Even if you believe that you're a positive thinker and have an overwhelmingly positive outlook, it may be worthwhile to ask a couple of trusted friends for their opinion of your attitude.

Positive thinking and a positive outlook on life offer you a bounty of great rewards. Researchers continue to discover more about the effects of positive thinking and optimism on people's health. Health benefits that positive thinking may provide include the following:

- Statistically longer (and happier) lives
- Decreased negative stress
- Lower rates of depression
- Greater resistance to catching the common cold
- A greater sense of well-being
- Reduced risk of death from coronary artery disease
- Easier breathing if you have certain lung diseases, such as emphysema
- Improved coping ability for women with high-risk pregnancies
- Better coping skills during hardships

It's unclear why people who engage in positive thinking experience these health benefits more than negative thinkers do. One theory is that having a positive outlook enables you to cope better with stressful situations, which reduces the harmful health effects of stress on your body. It is also thought that positive and optimistic people live healthier lifestyles: they get more physical activity, eat a healthier diet, and have reduced rates of smoking and alcohol consumption.[3]

Make Your Self-Talk Positive Too

Self-talk is that endless stream of thoughts that run through your head every day. These automatic thoughts can be positive or negative. Some of your self-talk comes from logic and reason, and other self-talk may arise from misconceptions you create because of lack of information.

If the thoughts that run through your head are mostly negative, your outlook on life is more likely to be pessimistic. If your thoughts are mostly positive or neutral, you're most probably an optimist: someone who practices positive thinking automatically. Overcome negative self-talk by recognizing it when it happens and replacing it with positive self-talk.[4]

Bottom line: Goals can be achieved. You're the only one who can write your goals down and make a personal commitment. Don't blame others for your own life and how it turned out: it is entirely and exclusively up to you!

◆ ◆ ◆

It's *your* life. Learn it. Live it. Love it!

CHAPTER 3

◆ ◆ ◆

WHAT PROSPECTS VALUE

What we obtain too cheap, we esteem too lightly: 'tis dearness only that gives everything its value.[1]

THOMAS PAINE

◆ ◆ ◆

Sell a client for a lifetime, not for the day.

WHE POWER OF UVP

I was associated with one of the most powerful legal research and data management companies in the world for four and a half years. As in most companies I have worked for, over time the quota went up, up, up and the sales professionals' income went down, down, down.

We were strongly positioned in the market and had a captive target market because we sold information and websites to attorneys. If you want to learn how to handle objections, try selling to an attorney. Everything they say is an objection! I sold websites to attorneys, and selling websites has never been easy, especially in the 2001–2004 time frame, when everyone and his brother were targeting websites and market share in the attorney space.

Our company had to be unique and have a solid product offering: a turnkey solution for an attorney's practice with very little involvement on the attorney's side.

My first message was simple:

> Mr./Ms. Attorney, I am _____ from _____.
> We provide you a turnkey web solution that reflects the character
> of your unique practice with minimal time commitment on your
> part, and we back it up with our 135 years of credibility, documented
> usage (stats), and give you preferred position on the number one
> site ahead of your competitors when searching for an attorney.
>   I have your biographical profile as _____. [Pass to
> them or confirm over the phone.] Is this correct? Great! That's all I
> need to get started, and I will send you a draft of the site that we
> will review together.
>   How's next week at this same time?

Then I said nothing. Silence is the most powerful tool you have;
practice it!

This was my opener. I had very little time to connect and make
a statement. I had less than a minute on average. I had to be overprepared and have my message down cold. That's where the UVP—your
unique value proposition—is parlayed into an appointment.

I could have said:

> "Hi, I am _____from _____. We sell websites, and I
> would like to set up a 45-minute consultation with you to learn
> more about your practice. . . ."

This little speech would have been quickly followed by a click of
the phone or the infamous slam of the door.

Here's why. The second pitch does not sound unique; it has no
credibility and clearly shows that I did not study my prospect. No attorney is going to give you 45 minutes after hearing that pitch. However,
an attorney will give you 60 seconds right then if you're clever enough
to grab his or her attention.

Let's do the math. An attorney makes upward of $200 per hour,
so why should he meet with you and lose $200? Your value had better

be more than $200 to get that first meeting. That's why it's critical to have your UVP down cold.

Now I ask you: What are *you* worth per hour?

Keep the above dollar amount in mind when you're making calls and presenting solutions. Your hourly amount will keep you more motivated and also more focused on real prospects versus tire kickers. I see it time and again: sales professionals wasting a ton of time with the wrong prospects. Your time is just as valuable as that of a lawyer who bills out at $200 per hour.

WHAT ARE YOU SELLING?

Regardless of your company's size and its product or service, you are responsible for selling. If you can't readily identify exactly what you're selling and why your customers are buying it, you will have a difficult time identifying prospects and setting appointments to sell to them.

Here's a hint: the answer to what you are selling extends far beyond the items on your brochure of services or your product line.

Call your most recently closed client and ask her why she bought from you. Use this information in your next sales call.

UNDERSTANDING USP AND UVP

There are two invaluable concepts you must master to understand what you're really selling and what your customers are really buying from you: your *unique selling proposition* (USP) and your *unique value proposition* (UVP).

Your USP is what is unique about the service or product you provide, in essence, the unique advantages you offer the customer. When talking about your product or service, your salespeople will emphasize the features and functions that create USP, differentiating your product or service from the competition's offering.

Your UVP is the specific value or benefit for the specific customer or prospect to whom the service or product is being offered: the overall package as it benefits or helps the recipient. The UVP communicates emotional attachments. It's peace of mind, elimination of problems, retention of experienced staff, tenure of a team, knowledgeable customer service—all the softer intangible elements or characteristics that help a prospect choose one company over another for the same product or service.

Also, remember that your UVP as perceived by one customer may not be the same as your UVP identified by another customer. It's up to you to know what unique value propositions may be valued by your target market and to emphasize them as variables in speaking with different members of your target market.

For example, children love going to McDonald's because of the toys in their Happy Meals and the in-store playgrounds; they also may care about the food they're given to eat, within reason. Parents love McDonald's because they can get free Wi-Fi indoors and low-priced reasonably nutritious food quickly without getting out of the car when they're in a hurry.

Two radically different UVPs for the same place, each totally valid for that particular target audience. How profitable do you think McDonald's would be if the kids didn't enjoy going there and getting toys in their Happy Meals?

For another example, let's look at the automaker Volvo. On the Volvo website, www.volvo.com, they describe their business like this: "Volvo provides transportation related products and services with focus on quality, safety and environmental care."[2] That's Volvo's USP, its unique selling proposition.

Although some people in these changeable times might buy a Volvo for its fun-to-drive factor, fast acceleration, and fuel efficiency, historically people have purchased Volvos for safety. In most consumers' minds, that's the Volvo's UVP, the unique value proposition that the company has emphasized in its marketing and selling materials.

It is very likely that your customers see value in your company, service, or products where you don't. You may be too close to it. Perhaps they appreciate the attention to detail you give them or the vibe of your company culture. Maybe it's your location, convenience, expertise, friendliness, reputation, price, knowledge, visibility, or sense of cool or their frustration with a competitor. You need to know their reasons for choosing you—how they benefit from doing business with you—so that you can strengthen your selling approach to your next prospects by incorporating those factors.

Leading with your UVP in your SMART Prospecting script is likely to be the golden key you need to unlock more appointments, more sales, and more income.

UNCOVERING YOUR USP AND UVP

Here's a bit of legwork to help you understand your company's USP and UVP.

If you don't have any idea of your company's (and your) USP and UVP, you might want to develop a short survey by using www.surveymonkey.com, www.freeonlinesurveys.com, www.kwiksurveys.com, or www.zoomerang.com.

On your survey, ask your customers these questions, at a minimum:

1. Why does your company do business with us?
2. What is your perception of our company?
3. How do you benefit from doing business with our company?
4. How do you benefit from doing business with me personally?
5. What could we do better to serve your needs?
6. What do you like most about our company?
7. What do you like least about our company?

Online Survey Resources

Here are some details on the online survey resources we just mentioned:

Survey Monkey (www.surveymonkey.com). All the Fortune 100 companies use Survey Monkey, and hundreds of thousands of individuals use its market research surveys before launching a new company, product, or service or before introducing new pricing. To use any of their expert survey templates, sign up for a Survey Monkey account, click on "Create Survey," select "Use an expert survey template," and browse to the template you would like to use.

Zoomerang (www.zoomerang.com). When the big decisions hang in the balance, the best businesspeople turn to market research to ensure that they make the right decisions. Data obtained from market research surveys augment gut reactions and anecdotal information to point to the best possible choices. Zoomerang is a division of MarketTools, one of the leading professional research companies in the world. That makes choosing Zoomerang to create, send, and analyze your market research surveys a smart choice.

With Zoomerang, all market research survey template questions are written by professional market researchers and can be customized to fit your needs. Pro and premium users have access to over 100 survey templates, and free basic users can get started with six core templates.

FreeOnlineSurveys (www.freeonlinesurveys.com). You don't have to be a web programmer to create a free online survey using their proprietary system. Part of what makes their online survey software so popular is the ability to create a survey in a matter of minutes regardless of your tech background. Most of their customers don't know any code.

To generate survey responses, you can choose to e-mail the survey, share a survey link (provided by FreeOnlineSurveys), or insert a small snippet of code on your website. Since the online survey collects all the data instantly, you can see survey responses in real time.

KwikSurveys (www.kwiksurveys.com). KwikSurveys is a free-to-use survey builder. The company designed KwikSurveys to be easy to use for people at all experience levels, and so you will quickly be creating surveys. Why is it free? Over 75 percent of their customers are educational and profit-free enterprises with little or no budget.

Your Results

- What is your company's USP?
- What do you sell that separates you from your competitors? What makes you unique in your marketplace?
- What's your company's UVP?
- Why do your customers do business with you? If you still don't know, call at least five current clients and ask them.
- What is your customers' perception of your company?
- How do your customers benefit from doing business with you?
- Describe in one sentence what you are *really* selling to your prospects.

Let's put all this together to focus on the buyer and create a universal value proposition that will resonate with your prospects and get you appointments:

"I help (target market) solve/receive (USP: their need/want) by (your selling statement) and (UVP: their benefit)."

Volvo example:

I help families with small children drive the safest car on the market by selling NHTSA's top automotive safety pick, the Volvo XC60, and providing families with driving peace of mind.

Let's use pizza as another example.

If pizza is the product, a gourmet pizza place might advertise its wood-fired pizza oven. The wood-fired pizza in our example is made from a recipe that the owner's Italian grandfather brought with him to Ellis Island from his bakery in Rome. That's the USP.

As you eat the wood-fired pizza at this gourmet pizza place, you listen to snatches of Italian conversations drifting from the kitchen, and your waiter, dressed in traditional European wait-staff attire, suggests a nice bottle of Chianti to enjoy with your meal. This is more than pizza; it's Italian authenticity, and it almost makes your mouth water to think of it. That's their UVP.

Button it up! Never leave a meeting with loose ends. Always take a few minutes to develop the next steps.

Your Turn

Now you try it:

1. Your target market
2. Your target's USP: need/want/pain
3. Your selling statement: product/service
4. Your target's UVP: benefit
5. Now write your UVP

Now write another version of your UVP. I want you to think and rethink, practice, and rewrite your UVP until you have it down cold.
Here are the next steps:

1. Run your UVP by a few of your most trusted and loyal clients. Practice on them to see what their feedback on your UVP is. Note it.
2. Reflect back to your client survey. Does your UVP match what your client survey results have shown?

Note. Depending on the way your target market is segmented, you may want to create a separate UVP statement for each market.

If you're having challenges coming up with your UVP or USP, ask your past clients a few questions:

1. Why did you buy from me?
2. Did you look at other companies before you went with me?
3. What was the unique difference between our offering and the offerings of other companies?
4. Would you refer us to others? Why or why not?

The results of this survey may surprise you.

Bottom line: If you smell, look, and sound the same as your competition, you *are* the same—at least to your prospects. If you're running around trying to sell without a UVP, stop immediately and work hard on crafting it. I will tell you right now that not having a well-prepared UVP is the core reason you're struggling at selling, because your prospect thinks you're the same as your competitor! You're not a commodity such as gas or water; you're a sales professional who probably is paid more than the average doctor or lawyer. Arm yourself with professional selling tools, starting with your UVP.

Now that you have created and internalized your UVP, put it into practice every day. Have your UVP written on a note card and read it aloud at night before you go to bed to make it part of your subconscious mind. The more you practice your UVP, the less you have to think about it. That gives you more time and energy to focus on asking your prospects powerful questions and listening to their true needs.

◆ ◆ ◆

Always go above and beyond. You'll always find yourself
alone in the "beyond" section.

CHAPTER 4

◆◆◆

READY, FIRE, AIM!

*The odds of hitting your target go up dramatically
when you aim at it.*

MAL PANCOAST

KNOWING YOUR TARGET market and spending time to refine your prospect list will save you many hours of time and frustration. Trust me on this. It's through our mistakes that we learn the most. When I first started my consulting business, I wanted to help small businesses grow. My vision was to give them all my knowledge and to work side by side with them to help them increase sales. I felt I could reduce the rate of small business failures while making an income for myself.

Knowing that my target market was small business, I immediately jumped in headfirst. I went to Chamber of Commerce meetings, every networking event east of the Mississippi, seminars, webinars, mixers, trade shows, conferences, presentations, and more. I developed and conducted seminars and webinars for small business owners. I invested in advertising, room rentals, coffee, and doughnuts.

Needless to say, I did it all, and I was exhausted. After all that work, I had made a lot of friends and obtained one paying client. I repeat: one paying client. Again, *one* paying client.

I remained positive. But all this activity was driving me insane. And borderline broke.

I took a large step back to reassess, knowing that sometimes when you are so close to the fire, you can't see the flames. In this case the flame was me; I was so consumed by my passion and vision that it never occurred to me that I was going after the wrong target. Over and over, the wrong target.

Albert Einstein once said that insanity is doing the same thing over and over and expecting different results.

I was going insane.

I was shocked to discover that no one wanted my advice or help with the exception of a very few. I was well known in my hometown of Rochester, New York, because of my marketing efforts, but I wasn't getting any traction outside my immediate network.

Here's what I found out about my prospects:

1. They were *too independent*. Entrepreneurs like to be their own bosses and will figure it out on their own—even if it means going bankrupt in the process.
2. They had *no money*. The entrepreneurs I was approaching had no extra money to pay a consultant. Sure, they would show up and drink my coffee and eat my doughnuts, but that was it.
3. I had *poor timing*. With the economy crumbling, even if they wanted to buy my services, they couldn't.
4. There's a serious *lack of understanding* of the value of a consultant. I still feel that people don't know what I do. The buying cycle is even longer when they have never used a consultant in the past.
5. Most important, *the problem was me*. I was so stuck on "this is my target" that I never took the time to really look at what I was doing and analyze it thoroughly. I thought, I can make this work no matter what. *Wrong*. No matter how hard you try, you can't fit a square peg in a round hole.

This is *your* time to look, listen, and study so that you do not make the same mistakes I made.

◆◆◆

You can never overprepare before a sales call.

Have a plan; here is a high-level overview of the consultative selling model:

SMART Prospecting:

- Develop leads and network.
- Identify the decision maker.
- Ask questions to identify needs.
- Ask for and set an appointment.
- Search for connections on LinkedIn.
- Leverage your current contacts and look for introductions.
- Enter into CRM (customer relationship management) to keep yourself organized.

Precall Preparation/Overcoming Objections:

- Identify the type of call and your purpose (purpose, process, and payoff).
- Research the business and its specific industry hot buttons.
- Create a list of open-ended questions, both broad and specific.
- Anticipate objections and think about ways to overcome them.
- Create an agenda.
- Always have a current agreement ready and on your person.

Opening/Overcoming Objections/Need Dialogue:

- Get to know them and their business.
- Introductions: your name, the company name, and what you do to build rapport. Compliment their business.
- State your purpose and use your agenda.
- Transition to a need dialogue.
- Surface needs and learn about their business: ask open-ended broad questions or use statements such as "Walk me through your current process." Identify additional decision makers.

- Overcome objections: acknowledge, ask questions, position your response, check for feedback.
- Close and recap: include actionable next steps.

Following Through:

- Follow up with the lead source.
- Send a thank-you card.
- Deliver on all your promises.
- Update CRM (action, results, etc.).

Closing/Solution Dialogue:

- Present proposal: solutions are customized to the prospect's needs and priorities.
- Review prospects' objections or ask what questions they have.
- Ask for the business.
- Negotiate.
- Discuss the next steps: set expectations for delivery time, follow-up, and outstanding items.

GOOD SELLING IS GOOD LISTENING

Listen with your eyes and ears: this is the most
fundamental secret to selling.

Once on my way home from Vancouver, I had to buy a last-minute souvenir and, of course, forgot to buy it before I got to the airport. I knew I wasn't going to be paying a reasonable price. I found the item I wanted to purchase, and a kind lady was cashing me out. She spoke broken English, but I was patient and friendly.

She asked me, "Where are you going, and how did you get here?" I was confused about the question; after all, I had already gone through customs, and this seemed out of the blue. I told her I was on my way to Rochester, New York, and then she asked again, "How did you get here?" I still was confused, and her English was hard to understand. I smiled and said, "Could you repeat your question?" She slowed down and said once again, "How did you get here?"

I said, "Taxi." She said, "That is the right answer!" She then told me she was delighted to give me a free gift valued at $16. I said, "Thank you! That is very kind of you. I would like to purchase this as well." She was surprised that I still wanted to purchase my original item because I had just won her gift. This created a win-win for both of us.

I guess the lesson I received from the experience is that many times people get defensive right off the bat in any communication interaction, even a trivial one at the airport gift shop. People raise their voices at each other when there is a language barrier (or perspective barrier) and practice zero listening skills. If you could slow things down just a little, *listen*, and smile, the world would be a much better place.

Practice active listening the next time you bump into a person who does not speak the same way you do and you might end up getting a free gift as well. At the very least you'll have an opportunity to practice your listening skills and learn something.

We have two ears, and one tongue, and so we can listen to prospects twice as much as we speak. That's how we learn about their needs and can decide how to best propose our product or service.

How well are you using the following good listening techniques?

- Stop talking.
- Don't interrupt.
- Empathize with the prospect.
- Ask clarifying questions.
- Be patient with the prospect's style and personality.
- Smile and respond appropriately.

- Evaluate the facts and evidence.
- Keep your emotions under control (especially anger and impatience).
- Focus only on the main points: the key ideas.
- Don't argue mentally.
- Listen for what *isn't* said.
- Listen to how something is said.
- Summarize key ideas often.
- Don't antagonize the speaker.
- Don't jump to conclusions.

◆◆◆

Ask questions and really listen to your prospect's answers.

START WITH THE END IN MIND

We're going to walk through this SMART Prospecting process together. You'll soon see how important it is to complete each of these steps if your goal is to improve your "sales sense" and, more urgent, close more business more quickly.

The Art of Closing by Listening

Many sales professionals dream of mastering the one-call close. The good news is that it can be done and you can learn the skill; all it takes is a little practice and application of the skill. Here is a step-by-step process for you to remember when trying to master the one-call close:

1. Refer to *Begin with the End in Mind* by Stephen R. Covey. Covey discusses imagination: the ability to envision in your mind what you cannot at present see with your eyes. His thesis is based on the principle that all things are created twice. There

is a mental (first) creation and a physical (second) creation. The physical creation follows the mental, just as a building follows a blueprint. If you don't make a conscious effort to visualize who you are and what you want in life, you empower other people and circumstances to shape you and your life by default. It's about connecting again with your own uniqueness and then defining the personal, moral, and ethical guidelines within which you can most happily express and fulfill yourself. Beginning with the end in mind means beginning each day, task, or project with a clear vision of your desired direction and destination and then flexing your proactive muscles to make things happen.

It's critical to begin with the end in mind. Every call you initiate in your mind and then in practice must be framed as "I'm going to close this person right *now*" rather than resigning yourself to follow-up calls and statement analysis.

2. *Active listening* is a communication technique that requires the listener to understand, interpret, and evaluate what she or he hears. The ability to listen actively can improve personal relationships by reducing conflicts, strengthening cooperation, and fostering understanding. When interacting, people often are not listening attentively. They may be distracted, thinking about another thing, or thinking about what they are going to say next (the latter case is particularly true in conflict situations or disagreements). Active listening is a structured way of listening and responding to others, focusing attention on the speaker. Suspending one's own frame of reference, suspending judgment, and avoiding other internal mental activities are important to fully attend to the speaker.

3. *Remain silent.* What you say is really not all that important; it's infinitely more important that the prospect feels that you are listening to her. Remind yourself to listen: active listening means your mind must be completely present and you must take an active role in the conversation. No thinking about your date,

last weekend's football game, or picking up your son for soccer practice.

Take notes. Doing that requires you to be engaged and listening to the prospect's needs. Don't finish other people's sentences; remain quiet and wait for the prospect to speak. Avoid being a silence filler; silence is an extremely powerful tool, and chattering too much derails your prospect's train of thought. The most important tip is to slow down. There's no need to rush. Remain in control throughout the conversation and let it unfold naturally. Practice patience with your active listening.

4. ABC: *always be closing.* Use words and statements such as "Today!" "Now!" "Right away!" "Fast and easy," "Let's go ahead today," "Business or personal checking account?" "Silence—pause—say nothing!" "All I need is your okay," "This makes sense, doesn't it?" "Let's get you started now!" "Seamless—no work on your end." "All I need to get you enrolled is an okay from you; now would you like me to send you an electronic copy of what we discussed or fax it to you?" (SILENCE.)

YOUR TARGET MARKET

A target market in the most general terms is a group of customers a business has decided is the most likely to purchase its products and/or services. Once a target market of customers is researched and defined, marketing and selling strategies can be developed that capture that audience's attention and ultimately convert those prospects into loyal customers.

The key here is to define the group of customers—your target market—to whom you will be making your SMART Prospecting calls.

Who are your current clients now? What common attributes do they possess?

WHY DEFINE A TARGET MARKET?

Ultimately, this step is necessary because you need to narrow your focus to a smaller target than every person and every company in the country (or the world). For example, as of 2009, there were about 27.5 million businesses of all sizes operating in the United States, according to the Office of Advocacy of the U.S. Small Business Administration.[1] Trying to reach all 27.5 million businesses is a time waster because only a small fraction of those businesses are likely to be qualified candidates for what you are selling.

Likewise, if you're selling to consumers rather than businesses, there are 311 million people in the United States, according to the U.S. Census Bureau.[2] Again, out of that huge number, only a small fraction is likely to fit the description of your target market.

Identifying your target market is the quickest and easiest way to focus on the companies or people most likely to be interested in purchasing what you are selling so that you can be more productive and earn more money faster.

HOW DO YOU DEFINE YOUR TARGET MARKET?

Let's start by creating an easy blueprint to get your target market tightly defined.

Target markets, whether made up of companies or consumers, have distinguishing characteristics that allow relatively easy segmentation, such as the following:

- *Location:* where people live or do business, such as all the delicatessens in Brooklyn or suburban commuters who use BART in San Francisco to travel to and from work
- *Demographics:* using measurable, easily available statistics such as industry, gender, age, income, and family life stage (empty nesters, newlyweds)

- *Psychographics:* shared strong attitudes, values, or lifestyles, such as achievers, urban dwellers, pet lovers, fun seekers, and creative types
- *Behavior:* based on lifestyles, disposable income, and spending habits, such as only buying American-made goods or consistently adopting new technologies first
- *Product-related:* name brand product loyalty, such as Starbucks customers, or use and consumption rates, such as drivers of pickup trucks compared with hybrid cars or motorcycles

If you sell business to business (B2B), you might use a combination of location and industry demographics, such as Standard Industrial Classification (SIC) and North American Industry Classification Systems (NAICS) codes to begin narrowing your target market.

In addition, check out www.manta.com,[3] which bills itself as the "world's largest online community for promoting and connecting small business." Currently, Manta is ranked as the third largest business news and research website by comScore and has an audience of 26 million people in the United States and around the globe. Companies list themselves for free and have opportunities to improve their free listings with advertising. What it provides you as a salesperson is a nicely segmented list of businesses to approach with your product or service.

Another great resource is www.salesgenie.com, which helps you identify quality business and consumer sales leads by using easy-to-tailor search tools. You can get a free three-day trial at their site to see if their process works for you.

Hoovers (www.hoovers.com) is part of the Dun & Bradstreet family. They generate qualified lead lists for your target market of companies or consumers. They also offer several other business services. They have a free trial and demo offer at their site that might be worth considering.

If you're selling business to consumer (B2C), demographics, psychographics, and behavior may be the most helpful criteria to use in identifying a target market. Don't overlook the fact-packed value of the latest government census (www.census.gov) in helping you narrow your target market. You'll find many cuts of the data online at their site, and you can search their database if the frequently requested searches don't match your requirements. In addition, the U.S. Census Bureau offers periodic free seminars to teach people how to create queries in their databases, extracting only the information they need.

Data.com for Salesforce is another content-rich search portal that provides you with the most complete and accurate company and contact data you'll find in one place. Sales and marketing pros get instant access to every detail they need to plan territories, build highly targeted lists, and gain actionable insights into people and companies. The data is always up to date because it's in the cloud, and it's only a click away because it's inside Salesforce.

Infofree.com can give you unlimited sales leads, mailing lists, and e-mail lists. Select, search, and download hundreds of databases and save thousands of dollars.

Other helpful resources for tracking down target businesses as well as individuals include local Chambers of Commerce, public records at town halls, and indexes and reference books at libraries. Also, consider the organizations and professional associations in which your target market may participate.

This is not to ignore social media connections such as LinkedIn and Facebook. LinkedIn has a search tool that allows you to look for a particular company (when you drill down that far in your target market) and find the person with the job title you need to call.

LinkedIn Groups are a hidden bonanza. Go to the LinkedIn drop-down menu in the upper right corner of your LinkedIn home page, select Groups, and then search for groups within your target market. Odds are good that the executives in your target companies are members of professional groups on LinkedIn. *All* the Fortune 500 companies are represented within LinkedIn Groups. LinkedIn Groups is where you can find common ground with your prospects and leverage the information to obtain an appointment.

In addition to finding your target company's executives in LinkedIn Groups, you can join and participate in the groups, providing yourself with more common ground on which to base your relationship with the executives.

If you have the budget, Facebook and LinkedIn allow you to purchase ads that come up right in front of your prospects. For $1.00 a day, Facebook will allow you to advertise in a way that truly targets your prospects. For $10.00 a day, LinkedIn does the same thing. Both LinkedIn and Facebook allow you to take a tour for free and see how many prospects are out there and then decide whether to purchase an ad.

Facebook strives to show relevant and interesting advertisements to you and your friends—and your prospects. Here are the facts about Facebook ads:

- Ads generally appear in the right-hand column of pages throughout Facebook. Ads are eligible to appear on many types of pages, including apps, photos, groups, pages, profiles, and the home page.
- The content of a Facebook ad is sometimes paired with news about social actions that your friends or prospects have taken (e.g., liking a page).
- Your friends may see news about the social actions you have taken in Facebook ads. This news will be shown only to your confirmed friends and will adhere to the applicable privacy settings you've set for your account. If a photo is used, it is your profile photo, not one from your photo albums.
- Facebook doesn't sell your information to advertisers.
- Facebook actively enforces policies that help protect your experience with third-party applications and ad networks.

LinkedIn Ads is a self-service advertising solution that allows you to create and place ads on prominent pages on the LinkedIn.com website. People click on your ads and visit your website. You specify which LinkedIn members view your ads by selecting a target audience: by job title, job function, industry, geography, age, gender, company name, company size, or LinkedIn Group. You can control your advertising costs by setting a budget and paying only for the clicks or impressions that you receive.

Virtually every profession and job title has a professional association, and you can search databases to find members and their contact information. For example, the American Medical Association has a DoctorFinder function that is searchable by specialty, city, and state. If you're not sure of the name of a professional organization or association, do a quick search on Google and see what you find.

In fact, you might also want to refer to the Directory of U.S. Associations to find the name of 60,000 business, professional, and trade associations (as well as 501c nonprofit organizations, charity institutions, and community institutions) operating in the United States.[4] The site claims to have more than 98,000 association executive contacts in its database.

JUST HATCHED?

If your company is a start-up or you want to expand your network, call your competitors. Yes, call them! They were just like you at one point, and so they may be past their growing pains and may hand you the small stuff they don't want to deal with anymore. You might be surprised by the outcome of the meeting: people want to help people, and if the chemistry is there, they will help you. What's the worst thing that could happen? They tell you no. Some will, some won't—so what?

◆◆◆

If you want to be in the top 10 percent, you can't be doing what the other 90 percent are doing. Create and follow your own road map to success.

THE PARETO PRINCIPLE

Pareto's familiar 80–20 rule holds here: roughly 20 percent of your customers generate about 80 percent of your revenue. Analyze the top 20 percent of your existing customers to understand their purchasing history and characteristics; then find prospects whose characteristics parallel theirs. These should be your top prospects.

If your company is a brand-new start-up, research any direct competitors and analyze their target market by using their websites, press releases, news journals, case studies, and other publicly available information. Compare what you find against the questions below.

Assuming that your company is not a brand new start-up, you should look closely at the customer files to answer the questions below. This information is important because you want to spend your time on the top 20 percent of your prospects:

- Which customers are purchasing regularly, and how large are their orders?
- How much is each customer purchasing, and how often?
- Which customers have purchased from you only once?
- Which customers have stopped buying? (Have you asked them why? There is gold in asking this question. Don't be afraid to ask why they stopped buying; in fact, they may be flattered that you asked. It shows you care about their business and have noticed that it stopped.)

Your Target Market Action Plan

Take these steps and ask yourself these questions:

1. Are you selling business to business (B2B) or business to consumer (B2C)?
2. Define your target market clearly.
3. What are the most distinguishing characteristics of your target market prospects? This list may include revenue, age, location, type of business, lead source, and so on. List at least four.
4. What is the buying process for your targets? Start at the top of the corporate ladder, not the bottom.

5. Why are these companies or consumers your best prospects? How do they look like or behave like the top 20 percent of your existing customers? Quantify how much business they could reasonably do with you (or how much current customers like them have done).
6. List your top five resources for finding and naming your target market candidates, such as trade journals, networking contacts, local or regional newspapers, LinkedIn, Google+, company websites, and Twitter.

FINDING THE DECISION MAKER

Now you have a great list of qualified companies in your customer relationship management (CRM) database to approach to set up appointments. The next step in narrowing your target market is to determine who the decision maker is whom you need to speak with when you are ready to set up the appointment. This will take a bit of investigation.

Check the company's website and see if it lists the title and/or name of the executive most likely to handle your product or service. Although there may not be a staff directory, check press releases, annual reports (if the company is publicly held), or product development information to sleuth around for names. Also, look through newspaper and business journal websites to see if there have been interviews or profiles done on the company or senior executives from which you can glean the names. Check LinkedIn, Facebook, Twitter, Plaxo, Google+, and YouTube for company pages and posted videos. These could also give you good leads deeper into the company, leads that don't take you through the front door and right into a gatekeeper.

If these resources aren't fruitful, it's time to pick up the telephone not for an approach call but for a fact-finding information call. Chapter 5, "Cultivating Great Bedside Manners," will show you how to create the right call messages.

You know what makes your organization unique. You've identified why your customers value your products over those of the competition. With those fundamental but critical items in place, you're ready to focus on your customers. Are you clear on which customers are your best ones? Crystal clear?

As a general rule, you want to spend about 80 percent of your time on the clients who are the most profitable and who embrace your reason for existence. This usually works out to be the top 20 percent of your customers. These are the people or companies that will give you the largest profit margin for your efforts.

There are other benefits to identifying your top 20 percent. Now you can confidently implement strategies that will let you:

- Eliminate spending too much time on those who give you the least amount of return for your effort.
- Create targeted marketing campaigns for specific customer categories.
- Establish incentive programs to move less active customers into your top range.
- Develop a relationship package to secure relations with your most valued customer groups (such as bronze, silver, gold, and platinum levels).

You can also assign sales and marketing specialists to focus on specific aspects of your customer segments. These specialists can include someone dedicated to the large accounts and strategic alliances, a relationship manager responsible for managing current clients and upselling, and a hunter who looks for new business where no current relationship exists between a customer and your organization.

To identify your top 20 percent, you first must segment your customers into niche categories. It's quite possible to have multiple categories, each with its own top 20 percent. Here are 20 questions to help you segment your existing customers into categories.

TWENTY QUESTIONS FOR IDENTIFYING YOUR STAR CLIENTS

◆ ◆ ◆ ◆ ◆

1. Where is the revenue coming from? What line item?
2. What are your customers passionate about?
3. What sales give you the greatest profit margins?
4. How do they pay? Credit, cash, corporate account, checks, PayPal?
5. Where do they purchase: brick and mortar, online, catalog?
6. What do they purchase? Which services? Which products?
7. What are their purchasing patterns? Once a year, many small items, a few larger items?
8. Where do they live? In an apartment, condo, city, suburb, development, out of state?
9. Where do they work? In a home office, downtown, office park, mom-and-pop store?
10. What personal attributes do they possess: consistent, fickle, committed, particular, loyal?
11. What types of people, places, and things do they like?
12. What do they value in their professional life?
13. What do they read?
14. When do they read it?
15. Where do they read?
16. What types of meetings, groups, or classes do they attend?
17. What do they value personally: education, money, service, philanthropy?
18. Which customers complain the most? About what?
19. What else do they purchase? From whom?
20. What type of people are you attracting to your business?

TEN EASY STEPS TO FINDING A CEO BY USING SOCIAL MEDIA

◆ ◆ ◆ ◆ ◆

1. Go to the prospect's company website and register for its newsletter to get up-to-date information.

2. On the company website's home page, look for social media links such as Twitter, LinkedIn, Facebook, and Google+, and join their accounts.

3. Go to LinkedIn and do a company search.

4. Search LinkedIn by the prospect's name and see how you are connected with her.

5. Reach out through your direct LinkedIn connections to get introduced to the CEO. When viewing the CEO's profile, look for common interests, groups, schools, books, or other indicators of common ground.

6. Go to Twitter.com and run a company search. If the company is listed, begin to follow it. Look at who your prospect's company is following. Develop or search for common interests so that you are prepared to converse with the CEO and establish rapport. Watch their tweets frequently as you continue your research.

7. On Twitter.com, also search for the CEO. If the CEO is listed, sign up to follow him. Look at who the CEO is following and find common interests so that you are prepared to converse. Monitor his personal tweets frequently to get a feel for what the person is thinking and saying. This will help in understanding his behavior style and personality traits, as was explored in Chapter 1 of this book.

8. On Twitter.com, search for groups that the CEO or the company follows as a member. Look at their tweets and learn more about what they are doing to develop common interests. Join any that you are interested in or that you think might be important to your prospect.

9. If they like your Twitter account, they will follow you.

10. If they follow you, you can then send them a direct message. Start by sending a personalized note, not a sales pitch.

Now you have a direct connection to your prospect.

Update your professional status often with new information, quotes, things you are doing, interesting news items, and so on.

Bottom line: You need to be out there and visible in cyberspace. Fill out your profile on LinkedIn and start making connections. Fill out your profile to 100 percent completion. Open a Twitter account, follow your prospects, and look for relevant information to leverage in future meetings.

◆◆◆

Your absence on LinkedIn only leads to professional suspicion.

CHAPTER 5

♦♦♦

CULTIVATING GREAT BEDSIDE MANNERS

Traditional methods of sales prospecting are grossly inefficient.

JILL KONRATH, SALES KEYNOTE SPEAKER AND
AUTHOR OF *SNAP SELLING*

DEVELOPING YOUR APPROACH

When do pilots start thinking about their approach to their destination? Answer: before they take off.

When do *you* start thinking of your approach to an important sales call? I bet its minutes before or, worse yet, not at all. Preparing for the call is the most critical aspect of a face-to-face call.

Here are the stories of three sales clowns using old-school techniques:

Sales Clown 1: No-Plan Stan. I was recently on a ride-along, and I asked him, "What is your plan on this call?" He quickly replied, "I don't know."

You have to have a plan; you need an agenda whether it is in writing or in your mind. Today's busy prospects have zero time for casual meetings: they want a purpose, a process, and a clear payoff.

Sales Clown 2: No Questions Please. I was with another salesperson, and he headed me off at the pass. I usually start with a "tell me more about the accounts we will visit today" question, but he started by saying, "Mike, I was thinking of questions you might ask me today, and you probably would like to know more details about the calls we have today, correct?" I said, "Yes." "Mike, it then occurred to me that I have *no idea* about these accounts I've been visiting for over two years. I know some personal information and contact information, but that's all."

Your clients want *you* to discover their true challenges at their businesses. Time after time a client thinks she wants ABC, and if the sales professional is doing the job well, the client ends up with XYZ. Think through and write down the questions you need to ask your prospects about their situation before every call. Create an intake sheet (see Chapter 9, "Soup to Nuts") that helps focus the meeting and get the information you need to help them get the right solution.

Sales Clown 3: Here's My Brochure. I was accompanying another salesperson on a call. We were out in his car for a moment before the call, and I asked him, "What's your plan?" The salesperson responded, "Mike, I've been selling for over 30 years, and I know what I'm doing. I don't need your help." I said, "Okay, thank you. Please do not lead the call with your brochure: ask some open-ended questions to get the prospect talking." He roared back, "I never lead with a brochure!" I responded, "Great." And we walked into the sales call.

The very first thing he did—even though we had just talked about it—was lead with his fancy (useless) brochure. The client was instantly bored and irritated at having her time wasted. Now I was faced with having to save the call, or what I call triage. I glanced over and noticed that the client's screen saver was displaying a flashing sports car motif, and I said, "Do you like cars?" The client said, "I love cars, Mike. Are you a car guy?"

I said, "I'm a car guy; I love cars!" She smiled and said, "Follow me."

We followed the client to her private climate-controlled garage tiled with an immaculate black-and-white floor. There sat eight Corvettes, three Ferraris, and two Lamborghinis. I was in heaven. Oh, yeah: the 30-year veteran sales professional quit later that day.

Sales is about people; it always has been and always will be. Stop talking and start asking open-ended questions. *Never* lead with a brochure, always plan, and have a few awesome thought-provoking questions ready to ask.

Whether you're picking up the telephone, sending a letter, meeting in person, sending a webinar invitation, inviting a connection through LinkedIn, or composing an introductory e-mail, you have 3 *seconds* to get your prospect's attention and 30 *seconds* to communicate your value proposition in a way she can instantly understand. Therefore, the way you approach your target that first time is essential to generating successful appointments with prospective customers.

When you're creating your approach, probably the most important thing to remember is that the prospect does not care about you or your company. Approaching your prospects is all about *them* and their needs or points of pain.

Park your sales spiel (and your ego) outside and put the prospect front and center. Resist the urge to turn every comment back to you, your company, and your products in an attempt to build rapport. It isn't perceived by the prospect as rapport building; it's seen as grabbing the "it's all about me" spotlight. There may be a time for that once you have sufficient information about the prospect and her pain. Focus on the prospect and everything you can learn about her.

Now we're moving into the meat of the SMART Prospecting process. You know with whom you need to speak, and you're ready to start making your calls and communicating your rehearsed messages.

NO SUCH THING AS A COLD CALL

This could be the start of a beautiful relationship. Although technically you may be calling people you don't personally know, there's nothing cold about these calls. Your prospects have a family, they hate broccoli, they work hard, and they look forward to weekends, pickup basketball games, and vacations just as you do. Will Rogers famously said that a stranger is just a friend you haven't met yet. Therefore, whether it's on a voice mail, in an e-mail, or during a live conversation by telephone, you want to sound friendly, approachable, and sincere without getting creepy.

Tone on the Phone

◆◆◆

Your tone is your appearance on the phone.

Try these great tips that I recommend to all the sales professionals I counsel. Place a mirror in front of you and have a glass of water nearby as you call. Do not drink while you are talking. Stretch before you sit down and do some light jumping jacks to get the blood going. All these small tweaks can make a difference in the way you present yourself over the phone.

Sit straight in your chair and focus on what you are doing. You are meeting people for the first time on the phone, and it's no different from meeting in person. The first impression is everything. Stand up or walk around when making calls and you will come across as energetic and interested. Close the door to your office (if you have one) to maintain silence around you. Add some light music in the background if you wish. No dogs, street noise, or doorbells. And please, no crying babies if you're working from a home office.

If you are typing notes into the computer as you talk to people, make sure you have a quiet keyboard. In the control panel settings for most computers, you can turn the clicking sound of the keyboard off completely. The other choice is to write your notes out longhand and then transfer them into your customer relationship management (CRM) system after the call concludes.

Tone is everything on the phone.

HAVE A PURPOSE

Every time you call a prospect, make sure you have a solid business purpose for calling and get right to the point. Although "how are you?" is polite, don't waste the prospect's time or yours with these niceties; skip it and get into your reason for calling. You want to invite the prospect to a product demo, set up an appointment, and ask clarifying questions to move the process forward in your most businesslike yet friendly manner.

Absolutely *never* call a target without a firm goal for that call in mind, one that you are ready to articulate crisply within the 45- to 60-second window, even on voice mail. Most voice mail systems are fairly sophisticated these days, and if you flub it the first time, listen to the prompts and rerecord your message if you can.

NURTURING LEADS

Sales are about getting the right message to the right person at the right time. That's why a sales cycle may take as long as a year, depending on the industry, the nature of your product or service, and the price tag. This means that you may go through this voice mail and e-mail appointment-setting cycle several times with Mr. Target before (1) he has the need or pain you can solve and (2) you catch his attention. The best perspective you can adopt is that each call and e-mail is a step in the right direction, taking you closer to your goal of landing Mr. Target and solving her pain. Persistence is your best friend.

However, there's a flip side to that coin: remember to cut your losses and move on if it's clearly a lost cause.

According to MarketingSherpa's B2B Marketing Benchmark Survey 2009,[3] the average sales cycle is between 1 month and more than 12 months, with the highest close rate between 3 and 6 months.

That study also revealed that approximately 40 percent of fresh leads moved from the initial inquiry to sales-ready and that same percentage advanced from sales-ready to qualified prospects. The trend deteriorated in moving from qualified prospect to converted to sale, with only 3 in 10 successfully converting.

My key message: don't expect overnight sales miracles like the ones you see in movies. That's Hollywood. This is the real world. You are on a long-term expedition that will pay great dividends if you invest the time. Be persistent, positive, and creative and you *will* make it to the top of the sales ladder.

TELEPHONE APPROACH

You should write your approach script of about 75 words so that it takes no longer than 45 to 60 seconds to recite in an unhurried, clear voice. It must not sound rehearsed, read, or canned or you will lose the prospect before you even get your three seconds. The most important thing is to start with a strong question or "grabber": something that makes the target think you have been inside his head or sitting on his shoulders, listening to what worries him.

To create an effective grabber, you must think about your target's perspective, understand what her business problems are, and know what you can do for her. Prospects are not interested in your company when you first get them on the phone, so put the focus on them and approach your products, services, and solutions from their perspective, not yours.

We will walk you through creating your complete script and messaging in the next few sections.

VOICE MAIL APPROACH

First, pay close attention to Ms. Target's outgoing voice mail message: is she on vacation or away at a conference? If she is out of the office for an extended time, perhaps you should find an alternative decision maker to approach or wait until Ms. Target is back in town so that you're not one of the dozens of calls she must do something about when she returns. Odds are good that she wouldn't call you in that case. Plus, if you leave a message asking for a meeting this week and she's gone for two weeks, you won't score very highly in listening skills.

Some executives leave messages that change daily, and others wouldn't know how to change their outgoing messages if their lives depended on it. Listen for verbal cues about your target's personality such as a regional accent, a lot of background noise, whether it was recorded by an administrative assistant, and whether the target sounds harried in the message. All of these things can give you some hints, making this person more three-dimensional and helping you find common ground and empathy as you create a relationship with this friend-stranger.

The voice mail approach is not very different from the live telephone call approach except that you need to speak your phone number and name twice slowly and clearly: once at the beginning of the call and once at the end.

E-MAIL APPROACH

Once you receive your prospect's e-mail address from the gatekeeper, a lead form, or your LinkedIn connection or by using the Email Checker application (www.ip-address.org/verify/email-checker.php), you have another great way to get Ms. Target's attention.

Further, you can alternate your voice mail calls with e-mail messages that reinforce what you have to solve her pain and make it more compelling for her to contact you. In your introductory e-mail, whether or not you have left a voice mail message, you'll want to use your 45- to 60-second telephone script and include a subject line that compels the person to spend the few seconds to open and scan your e-mail.

After you have your subject line carefully crafted (see below), you will adapt your telephone and voice mail scripts to e-mail. The good news is that you can use more words, but in essence, you want to reinforce the voice mail message you left as concisely as possible.

Approach Letter with or Without an Information Packet

As you might expect, your approach letter is crucial to paving the way for an appointment. As with all other areas of the sales process, it must set you apart, making your target remember you vividly and in a professional way. Here are some sales pro tips:

- Print your approach letter on real company stationery (not just 20-pound printer paper) and make sure to sign it personally in blue or black ink.
- Don't use a number 10 business-size envelope, those ubiquitous 4⅛-inch by 9½-inch envelopes that (among other things) bring us bills and IRS notices. Use an Executive or Monarch size (3⅞ by 7½ inch), a 6-inch by 9-inch, a 9-inch by 12-inch, a brown Kraft envelope: whatever you can find that is unusually sized or colored. Anything but a "normal" number 10 business envelope. Your approach and sales process with this decision maker should look anything but normal right from the beginning.
- Use real stamps for the envelope; it should not be metered and bar coded like every other piece of mundane mail that leaves your company each day.
- Handwrite the person's name and address on the envelope rather than printing it on a label.
- Go to the local office supply store and buy an ink pad (red is effective) and a stamp or a self-inking stamp that says "Priority," "Rush," "Confidential," or even "Urgent" to use on the envelope. Some schools of thought hold this to be an archaic technique

that has lost its power to impress. Consider it within the complete context of your sales approach and try it to see if it works for you. If it does not, you're out only the cost of an ink pad and stamp.

- If getting into this account merits it, consider upgrading to an overnight envelope sent using a U.S. Postal Service priority mail flat-rate envelope, Federal Express, DHL, or UPS. The cost of this service is minuscule compared with the attention you'll receive and the opportunity you are opening. The same caveat applies here as in the prior point. Some regard this as hokey, but depending on your products or services, it's worth giving it a try.

- Send something of value with the approach letter whether it's a trade show giveaway, a recent white paper on a relevant subject, a clipping you found about the company in a recent newspaper or magazine, or a product demo DVD to increase your value in the target's eyes, so that he recognizes your name and welcomes your call.

- Make your approach personal. If you can glean any information from Facebook, LinkedIn, Google+, or other online sources about your prospect's outside interests, use it to make your approach personal and unforgettable. It doesn't have to be big, but it does require some thought and research, going beyond the run-of-the-mill sales approach.

One sales professional I know found his target executive on LinkedIn and discovered from his profile that he loved fly fishing. He bought an inexpensive fly fishing kit, sent it along with his approach letter, and opened that door with a little thought and effort to capture a big account.

Another sales professional, this one a financial advisor, saw an article about a local lottery winner with whom she was slightly acquainted. She bought a nice frame and had the newspaper article about the lottery winner's windfall framed professionally and then sent it to him along with an introductory letter. The lottery winner had many other financial advisors approach him, but none with a unique approach like this one.

At the holiday season, one creative sales professional sent a remote control toy to her top prospects but did not send the remote control with the toy. The letter accompanying the toy told the executives they would get the remote control at their first appointment.

I set up an appointment with a CEO of a large marketing firm through LinkedIn. She stated, "I usually do not set up appointments with sales consultants, but I noticed you were reading the same book as me, so how's your calendar to meet?"

Bottom line: Start your approach early in the sales process; you have only one chance to make a first impression. Remember: your prospects are looking for a reason *not* to buy from you, and every little detail counts or hurts.

Be a sales maker, *not* an order taker.

CHAPTER 6

◆ ◆ ◆

CIRCLING THE WAGONS

◆◆◆

You have to be delicately irritating to get in front of a prospect.

Originating in the Old West, where pioneers would circle their wagons for protection from attack, this strategy is about looking for protection and getting defensive and ready for an attack.

You as a sales professional need to break that circle and get inside your prospect's circle. You need to use any means possible to "attack" the prospect, create a tremendous amount of value, and ask for the appointment.

Think back on all the people in your life and when you first met them. Did you immediately hit it off, or did it take some heavy lifting to make it work? And if it did take some heavy lifting, was it worth it?

More than likely, you just clicked. Your prospects want to click with you as well. They do not want to work hard on the relationship; they want it to be easy to work with you and want you to solve their problems quickly.

I was listening in to a sales professional on the phone, and it was painful to hear how hard the prospect was trying to give that person money and buy her service. The sales professional wasn't getting the message and was her own worst enemy. Are you your own worst enemy?

I was on a sales call with a different sales professional, and he did an awesome job. It was a perfect call: the prospect was engaged, happy, and ready to buy. I was excited that the sales professional was going to get the sale and was thinking to myself, With such a great approach, why is this sales professional behind on quota?

Then the strangest thing happened in the call. The prospect asked, "Where do I sign, and when can we get started?" I was thrilled because to me, when a prospect says that, we have had a perfect call. There was little the sales professional could do at that point *not* to get the sale and blow this golden opportunity.

Instead, the sales professional responded, "Maybe you should think it over; it's a big decision!" I almost fell out of my chair in pure shock. Ms. Prospect then said, "You're right; maybe we are rushing into this." Long story short: the prospect never signed up, and I found out why this sales professional never made quota. Sad.

The number one reason a sale does not close is that the sales professional does not ask. Are you asking for the business, and do you believe in your product or service? If not, you will never be successful in selling. Find something you are passionate about, ask for the business, and you will be successful.

◆◆◆

Passion + asking = sales success

THE NUMBERS

You signed up to be a sales professional, yet most salespeople are unsuccessful; that's the sad truth. You must be driven, self-motivated, ready to build great relationships, and organized. Let's start from the top and work our way down in mapping out your territory.

The numbers have not changed since the caveman sold the first wheel to his prospects. If the caveman set 10 appointments in a week, he would get three viable opportunities and sell one new wheel. What happened to the other seven? A lot happens to the other seven, and it can be very frustrating to you as a sales professional to maintain a positive attitude when seven appointments canceled or were not there when you showed up. Some of them will reset to another week, and many, sadly, will never reset, and you will have to go back and play the never-ending game of cat and mouse that we all love. *Not!*

So, what can you do to handle your losses? Follow the sales process perfectly. Why? Because it's built around the numbers, and the numbers do not lie.

Example: You have a territory of 500 accounts to market to in a calendar year, in other words, 500/50 working weeks in a year = 10 new prospects to approach each and every week. Out of those 10, 3 will be engaged, and at a 33 percent close ratio, one new sale will happen.

If one sale equals $2,000 in commission, you will make over $100,000 in a year. Do you want more income? Increase the number of the prospect letters you send out every week. That's the great part of being in sales; you alone have the opportunity to create your own income in comparison with the opportunity the average employee has for overtime hours or a bonus to increase her income. Hope is never a profitable strategy in predicting one's income. That's like hoping you will win the lottery, and we all know the odds on that.

Your turn:

Number of prospects in your territory _____
divided by working weeks in a year _____
equals the number of _____ prospects per week you need to
   approach.

How much do you want to make this year? How many sales do you need to make to meet that income goal? How big is your territory? How many prospects are there in your territory?

TIMING

I use to get into discussions with my managers about timing and how they felt that I was not asking the right questions or that something was wrong in my process. Being who I am, I would always challenge back in a polite professional manner and talk about timing: "It's not the correct time yet for XYZ."

Here is the sad truth: no matter how great you are in sales or how bad you are in sales, it always boils down to having the correct decision maker, a great value-based message, and perfect timing. No matter how hard you push or leverage any selling techniques, until the stars are aligned and the timing is correct for the prospect, it will be very hard to sell to that prospect. Some of you may disagree and be the exception to the rule, but it's not the norm.

We all have met a horrible sales professional who always seems to have dumb luck, and it drives the rest of us crazy. You know who I'm referring to: the person who just seems to fall into an account that makes his year. Peel back the onion and examine what happened behind the sale and I bet you will find that the sale was in progress many years before, and he just happened to stumble into it at the right time. That's how powerful timing is in the sales process.

Guess what? When the timing is right, more than likely your prospect won't negotiate or play any games because her need supersedes the cost. It's a beautiful thing when that happens, but it's rare.

Your overall prospecting approach has a specific cadence to it and will occur over a period of about five to seven workdays. Follow my proven formula and you'll have more appointments (and more sales) than you ever thought possible.

Figure 6.1 shows how the SMART Prospecting process works. We examine this diagram further in Chapter 9.

WEEKLY CALENDAR

The SMART Prospecting process is spread out over a one- to two-week period. Let's take a look at my calendar for a typical five-day workweek. For the sake of this example, let's assume that this is my first week on the job and therefore no past prospecting and SMART Prospecting have occurred.

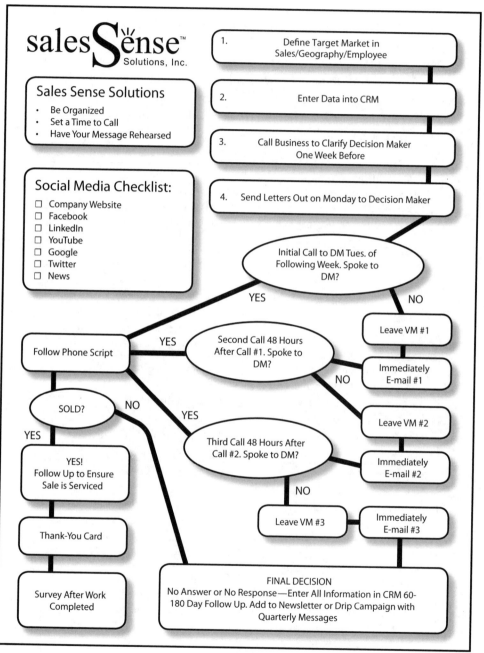

FIGURE 6.1

Of course you are doing much more during these days than just prospecting for new appointments. This is the portion of your day you've set aside to prepare for the next wave of appointments and sales calls.

We're talking about the perfect sales week. Goal: one or more new sales, 10 phantom appointments, 10 in-person appointments, and setting up campaigns. The chart below is based on 10 new prospects per week. If your territory is larger, increase your calendar times.

Monday morning Mail letters to new campaign Research future campaigns Call gatekeepers to clarify decision makers and contact information	**Monday afternoon** 1:00 2nd call appointment 2:30 2nd call appointment 5 after 5* Plan and set up the next day
Tuesday morning 8:00–9:00: phantom appointments 10:00: 1st call appointment 11:30: 1st call appointment Try my luck with drop-ins	**Tuesday afternoon/evening** 1:00: 1st call appointment 2:30: 1st call appointment 4:00 and beyond: 2 or 3 call appoint- ments and follow-up calls 5 after 5* Plan and set up the next day
Wednesday morning 8:00–9:00: phantom appointments 10:00: 1st call appointment 11:30: 1st call appointment Try my luck with drop-ins	**Wednesday afternoon/evening** 1:00: 1st call appointment 2:30: 1st call appointment 4:00 and beyond: 2 or 3 call appoint- ments and follow-up calls 5 after 5* Plan and set up the next day
Thursday morning 8:00–9:00: phantom appointments 10:00: 1st call appointment 11:30: 1st call appointment Try my luck with drop-ins	**Thursday afternoon/evening** 1:00: 1st call appointment 2:30: 1st call appointment 4:00 and beyond: 2 or 3 call appoint- ments and follow-up calls 5 after 5* Plan and set up the next day
Friday morning Follow up on all activity from the week Send handwritten thank-you notes Set up for next week and make sure to have a full week of activity planned	**Friday afternoon** Paperwork and expense reports If you have made your goals, go have a lot of fun!

*Make five prospect calls after 5:00 p.m. on weeknights.

◆◆◆

It's the open, not the close, that sells the prospect.

---

5 after 5 is one of the most critical activities of the sales week. I've had my best luck calling chief executive officers (CEOs) and chief financial officers (CFOs) after five at night. There is no gatekeeper in your way, and the executives usually pick up their direct lines.

Trying one's luck with drop-ins is another tactic that is very powerful when planned and executed correctly. Here is how it goes: during your 5 after 5 calls, you hit their voice mail and leave a message like this:

"Hi, _____ [Prospect]. This is _____ [Your Name] at _____ [phone number]. I know we keep missing each other by phone. It just so happens that I will be in your area around _____ [time you will be in the area] tomorrow, and I'm going to try my luck and drop in at your office so we can put a name with a face. I hope to see you tomorrow for a brief moment, and then we can set up something more formal. Have a great evening!"

Next day:

You stop by at the time you promised at his or her office and are greeted by the receptionist/gatekeeper. What do they always say? You guessed it: "Are they expecting your call?" You can proudly say yes with a small grin of pride.

It's important to defuse or head off objections. There are many ways of getting around gatekeepers, and guess what? You just learned one. Practice makes perfect. Have this book with you the first couple of times until the whole process seems natural and comfortable.

The prospect will come out if you have followed my process and delivered value-based messaging and usually will apologize for not getting back in touch with you, because now there are no barriers between you and your prospect, no e-mail delete button or caller ID to get in the way. You're head to head with your prospect.

"Thanks for coming out to talk with me _____ [Prospect]. I was in the area as my message stated last night, and I wanted to set up a brief appointment to learn more about you and your current business challenges. How's next week on Tuesday or Thursday?" (Pause) Confirm the time and send out a calendar invite to the prospect immediately after you leave so that she knows it's important to you.

Start your Monday with a sales order: it will make you happy all week.

Phantom appointments by my definition exist only for you, not for the prospect. They are set appointments in your calendar (not the prospect's calendar) to make the phone appointments that you mentioned in your approach letter: you will be calling at that specific time, for example, Thursday at 8:10 a.m. You place each phantom appointment in your calendar at the precise time you stated you would call the prospect. Then do it.

In your calendar time slot you should have the following: name, title, company, phone number, e-mail, LinkedIn profile, notes, any news that you found to mention to the prospect, and maybe a curiosity statement.

Curiosity statements are statements that leave your prospect craving more information from you. Here's an example:

"Hi, _____ [Prospect]. This is _____ [Your Name] at _____ [phone number]. I just saw in _____ [article/news/web] that you _____ [fill in the blank]. We just helped a client in the exact same situation. Give me a call back when you return to your desk, and I can share some more information with you. Have a great day! Again, this is _____, and my phone number is _____."

Notice that I did not tell the prospect how we helped the referenced client. I just left a very simple message to create a ripple of interest and pique her curiosity.

There are three psychological elements you can use effectively in all sales conversations:

1. *Curiosity.* People are very curious by nature and always want to be in the know and away from the unknown.
2. *Self-preservation.* Our brains are built around protecting us. Either fear or greed will protect us and make us better or worse off, and we *never* want to be worse off. If you say something like "We have only two left at this price, and I'm not sure if we are getting any more in for a long time," your prospect is very likely to jump immediately at the offer because of his fear of loss or greed; he doesn't want to miss out.
3. *The takeaway.* My favorite is the takeaway, because we all want something we cannot have. The minute you take away your offer from a prospect, she will always want it more. I often use this technique when I meet a know-it-all or someone who is just downright rude. (I know; rudeness is a rare case in the world of human dynamics and selling.)

I simply say: "You know, [prospect name], I just don't think this service or product is right for you." (Long Pause) The prospect will think for a moment or two and then always say, "Why not?" I will say, "Well, it seems like it's just not a fit for you and your business. I know other companies [if you can, be specific and name one of their key competitors] that have been extremely successful in using this product or service, but it does not seem to be a good fit for you, and at this point I do not even know if you would qualify." They will immediately go into selling you on why they would qualify and how the product is perfect for them at this time. It's an amazing turn of events and frankly a lot of fun to listen to them selling you back on your own product.

Also notice that we send the letters out on Monday and then do follow-up calls starting on Wednesday. On average, it takes someone 2.1 days to return a call. This gives your prospects two days to pick up the phone to call you before you contact them proactively.

After three unsuccessful attempts to contact a prospect, if you have not connected with him, you will send him a final e-mail or give him a final call and then cut your losses and move on.

Hail Mary Moves

Here are three things you can do at the end of the process; these are known as the Hail Mary moves:

1. Send a calendar invite for a 10-minute phone appointment and see if the prospect accepts it.
2. Stop by the office in person.
3. Send a LinkedIn invitation to the prospect.

All three have worked for me after I've followed the SMART Prospecting process to the letter.

CALL AND CONTACT SEQUENCE

Here are the seven steps to follow:

1. Clarify data and set up a campaign for your letters and prospects in your customer relationship management (CRM) file.
2. Research your targeted 10 accounts by utilizing Google, LinkedIn, and Twitter.
3. Enter your 10 target accounts into Google Alerts and set the frequency to once a week for updates.
4. Call the gatekeeper/administrative assistant to clarify any information and state that you will be sending an important letter to his or her attention.
5. Send out the letter (hand addressed) on Monday in an urgent envelope (FedEx or DHL) or in a normal envelope with your value messaging and business card enclosed. Remember, it's about your prospect, not about you.
6. Set up phantom appointments in your calendar between 8:00 a.m. and 9:00 a.m., 10 to 15 minutes apart.
7. Timing: if your prospects are local, schedule calls three business days out from the approach letter. If your prospects are out of

town, adjust your schedule to up to five business days out. On all messages after the first one, set your callback schedule for two business days. Alternate between morning and afternoon; if you called in the morning, try again in the afternoon, and vice versa. Remember to always include your 5 after 5 rule each day.

Here is an example of a call sequence:

Week 1, Monday: letter
Week 1, Thursday: phantom appointment message 1
Week 2, Monday: message 2
Week 2, Wednesday: message 3
Option after message 3: one of the Hail Mary moves

Follow this sequence:

1. Message 1: Voice mail 1 and follow it immediately with e-mail 1. (As promised in my letter . . .)
2. Message 2: 48 hours after message 1, leave voice mail 2 and follow it up immediately with e-mail 2. (Is there someone else . . .)
3. Message 3: 48 hours after message 2, leave voice mail 3 and follow it up immediately with e-mail 3. (I'm moving on; last chance to talk with me . . .)
4. Hail Mary move: Within 48 hours of message 3, send the prospect a calendar invite for a time or a LinkedIn invitation or stop by in person.
5. Live conversation with your prospect.

Return phone calls immediately. Once your client or prospect leaves a message, he or she is counting the minutes until you respond.

ALTERNATIVE METHODS

We will look closely at how to create compelling voice mail messages and then do the same for live conversations and e-mail messages. But first, let's look at some of the interesting technology options that are coming to market. These innovations may prove useful to you as you develop a creative sales process for approaching your prospects. One of them may help you create the ripples of interest and curiosity you need to get in front of a high-profile prospect.

TECHNOLOGY OPTIONS

Here are some of the many technology options available to you:

LinkedIn. This is the world's largest professional networking site, with more than 150 million professionals around the world. Members include executives from every Fortune 500 company, and so the odds are high that the executive prospect you are targeting is listed on LinkedIn. If she is, sending a request to connect is an effective way to get her attention.

Then you'll weave that connection into your overall approach.

Fax/PC fax. Just because these are somewhat older technologies, don't discount them in your sales prospecting. Some professions, such as attorneys, still use faxing heavily. As a way to get your target's attention, a well-timed fax may do the trick.

If you have a fax number, send your opening letter and initial messaging by fax. The nice part about using a fax is that a lot of people do not use it, and so you will stand out. The fax is usually hand delivered to the prospect by the mail room or is converted to an e-mail. When I was selling to attorneys, I would leave a voice mail, then send an e-mail, and then send a fax—all within two or three minutes. Try www.freefax.com, www.faxzero.com, or www.efax.com to fax directly from your computer.

Skype. I love Skype. What a great sales tool. If you do not have it yet, set it up today. You can send messages, talk, and share your desktop to conduct a presentation. You can also search for your prospects and connect by using Skype, and when a prospect logs on to Skype, you will see a message on your screen announcing that "XYZ is online." You can then attempt to connect with the prospect with Skype: "Send me an invite at Sales Sense Solutions."

Skype has text, voice, and video options to make it easy to connect with your colleagues and prospects in whatever format is easiest. You can make free telephone calls over the Internet, send texts, use instant messaging (IM), use your phone or computer, or connect by video conference. Best of all, its basic voice services are free.

FaceTime/Fring/Qik Video. FaceTime for Mac makes it possible to talk, smile, and laugh with anyone on an iPad 2, iPhone 4, iPod touch, or Mac from your Mac. The one drawback with FaceTime is that it's compatible only Mac-to-Mac devices. Fring and Qik Video work with Androids as well as other smart devices.

FreeConferenceCall (www.freeconferencecall.com). These conference calls are simple and easy to use, requiring only a name and an e-mail address to receive an instant account. You are then instantly provided with a dial-in number and access code for immediate phone conferencing. Your teleconferencing line is available to you 24/7, and there is no need to schedule or make reservations. Each conference call account accommodates 96 callers on an unlimited number of six-hour free conference calls.

Google+ (pronounced "Google plus") (http://plus.google.com). This is a Google social networking project. The Google+ design team sought to replicate the way people interact offline more closely than is the case in other social networking services, such as Facebook and Twitter. The project's slogan is "real-life sharing rethought for the web."

Twitter. Twitter is an online social networking service and microblogging service that enables its users to send and read text-based posts up to 140 characters long known as tweets. Frequent tweets from a company or salesperson keep awareness current and in front of the followers daily.

Twitter was created in March 2006 and launched that July. The service rapidly gained worldwide popularity, with over 500 million active users as of 2012, generating over 340 million tweets daily and handling over 1.6 billion search queries per day. Since its launch, the Twitter website has become one of the top 10 most visited on the Internet and has been described as the SMS [Short Message Service] of the Internet. Unregistered users can read tweets, and registered users can post tweets through the website interface, SMS, or a range of apps for mobile devices.

Texting. Maybe I'm still a little old school; I do not recommend texting until a firm relationship is established and you have asked permission to text as a form of communication. I will leave the decision to use texting on your sales approach up to you and your comfort level. Texting is probably not the best approach method early in a relationship with a new prospect, as it may feel to the prospect that you are (1) violating his personal life and (2) stalking him. Get to know the person a bit better before texting her. However, as Generation X and Y professionals (and eventually the millennial generation) become executives, you are likely to see texting establish more prominence in the business world.

Never text while driving, as it is illegal in most states as well as deadly dangerous.

Webinars or web conferencing. Webinar invitations are powerful. One of the best ways in which I promote myself and sell services is by offering webinars. This refers to a service that allows conferencing events to be shared with multiple remote locations. One great idea you can implement is to develop a webinar topic that is based on your product or company's value and collect information and follow up on it immediately after the webinar. You must stay away from too much of a sales pitch.

Two of the most prominent providers of web conferencing are www.gotomeeting.com and www.webex.com. Also check out www.freescreensharing.com.

Most vendors also provide either a recorded copy of an event or a means for a subscriber to record an event. These services allow information to be shared simultaneously across geographically remote locations in nearly real time. Applications for web conferencing include meetings, training events, lectures, and short sales presentations.

Some solutions require that additional software be installed by the presenter and participants (usually by download), and others eliminate this step by providing physical hardware. Most also provide a means of interfacing by e-mail and calendaring so that customers can plan an event and share information about it in advance.

Video presentations. YouTube dominates the world in video, and since the invention of the television, people have been trained to be glued to videos and actually pay attention. You can use PowerPoint and a tool such as Camtasia to record a minivideo of your services and send the prospect a link to view the video. Look for applications from vendors such as Brainshark and Camtasia. For example, with Brainshark's cloud-based solution you can easily transform static content such as PowerPoint and Keynote documents into voice-enriched online and mobile video presentations that can be accessed anytime on demand and tracked so that you can measure the effectiveness of your communications.

Applications. At Sales Sense, I've created apps for the Android and the iOS platforms (iPhone, iTouch, iPad) that provide an extensive array of strategies, tactics, and tools to help you with the selling process. These are free applications to enhance your selling success. If you have an application for your product or service, send your prospect a link to download and take a trial. It's a great way to get personal on their smartphone and begin the relationship.

Time Trade (www.timetrade.com). This is an enterprise-class online
appointment-scheduling application that lets businesses, individuals, and salespeople connect easily and quickly with prospects, accelerating the sales process. The scheduling software is
built on the flexible Appointment Cloud SaaS Platform, which
enables customized professional solutions fully integrated with
existing business processes and workflows.

TimeTrade's web-based appointment scheduling software for
sales teams does the following:

- Lets prospects book sales meetings at the height of their
  interest right from your website, landing page, or e-mail
  campaign.
- Helps you reclaim the time sales representatives waste on
  back-and-forth e-mails and phone calls to schedule sales
  appointments.
- Has been proved to improve close rates by 20 to 30 percent
  and reduce the sales cycle by 30 percent.
- TimeTrade lets appointment request recipients add a new
  appointment easily to a Google Calendar, Microsoft Outlook, Lotus Notes, iCal, and ICS without retyping.

Spoke (www.spoke.com). Spoke Software is the new source for
timely, relevant, and comprehensive information on companies
and people. It was designed from the ground up to meet the
needs of business managers and sales and research professionals.

Launching with an initial database of over 30 million
entries across hundreds of industries, Spoke Software helps
drive businesses forward with its robust crowd-sourced data-
gathering model, paired with automatically updated enterprise-
specific news. Business professionals turn to Spoke Software to
find the latest company information, including executive profiles, company milestones, industry trends, news, blog posts, and
much more.

Spoke Software also allows business professionals to create
user-friendly profiles of companies and people in a smooth and
organized process that replaces existing inefficient data-gathering

techniques. Profiles are shared with the community at large, including peers, partners, and industry experts; all are able to interact and collaborate to create relevant insights about people, companies, industries, and trends.

SalesForce.com mobile, SalesForce.com, Data.com, Jigsaw. These companies have combined into a powerhouse of business applications, including Salesforce CRM, business directories, contacts, and company information.

Salesforce is as easy to use as the websites you use every day. You can log in from anywhere, view and update customer data, and work with your colleagues any time you want. Import your existing data from Sage ACT, Gmail, or Outlook or upload an .XLS/.CSV from an Excel or Numbers file, and before you know it, you're ready to go. If you can click a mouse, you can change workflows, add fields, and create sales processes. The result? Higher productivity and automation like you've never had before.

Data.com. Contacts by Jigsaw is a business directory where you can find contact and company information. The directory has business contact information for private as well as public companies.

Every business contact on Contacts by Jigsaw is complete with e-mail, phone, and title. (No other business directory provides contacts with both phone and e-mail information.) They offer business contacts in any company at any department across any industry. Their mission is to map every business organization on the planet, contact by contact, and keep them current through a collaborative effort.

Spokeo (www.spokeo.com). This is the most comprehensive people search engine in the United States. The unique technology and sophisticated algorithms combine offline directory and demographic data with the most complete online social data set in the world. Spokeo gives the user flexibility to search for anyone by name, phone number, e-mail address, or online user name. Each profile contains detailed information, including address, phone number, e-mail address, gender, age, ethnicity, social network profiles, and more. Spokeo's technology has earned accolades and reviews from *Newsweek,* the *Wall Street Journal, TIME,* and *USA Today,* among others.

Email Finder.com. Find an e-mail address today. For everyone from former coworkers to old classmates, use this e-mail lookup to get back in touch. Email Finder.com's powerful reverse e-mail address lookup tool allows you to find information about long-lost friends or colleagues, including full name, current physical address, phone number, and even social network sites they are members of simply by entering an e-mail address in the Search by Email feature.

Zoho (www.zoho.com). Zoho provides CRM, with more than 25 ready-to-use apps supporting all aspects of your business, from getting more sales to getting paid and from supporting your customers to making sense of it all.

foursquare. foursquare is a location-based mobile platform that makes cities easier to navigate and more interesting to explore. By checking in via a smartphone app or Short Message Service (SMS/texting), users share their locations with friends while collecting points and virtual badges.

foursquare guides real-world experiences by allowing users to bookmark information about venues they want to visit and by surfacing relevant suggestions about nearby venues. Merchants and brands leverage the foursquare platform by utilizing a wide array of tools to obtain, engage, and retain customers and audiences.

Pinterest. Pinterest is a virtual pinboard that lets you organize and share all the beautiful things you find on the web. People use pinboards to plan their weddings, decorate their homes, and organize their favorite recipes.

Best of all, you can browse pinboards created by other people. Browsing pinboards is an enjoyable way to discover new things and get inspiration from people who share your interests. Pinterest's goal is to connect everyone in the world through the "things" people find interesting. The theory here is that a favorite book, toy, or recipe can reveal a link between two people. (I agree.) With millions of new pins added every week, Pinterest is connecting people all over the world on the basis of shared tastes and interests.

Focus (www.focus.com). Focus makes the world's business expertise available to everyone. At the heart of Focus is a network of thousands of leading business and technology experts who are thought leaders, veteran practitioners, and upstart innovators in hundreds of different topics and markets.

You can connect with the experts on Focus in three primary ways:

- *Q&A*. Focus Q&A provides business and technology professionals with an opportunity to ask questions of and receive multiple answers from Focus Experts. It's a great way to get nearly instant answers to specific business questions.
- *Research*. Produced by leading experts, Focus Research is designed to provide businesses with the knowledge and insight they need to make important decisions. Research offerings are often based on data collected from Focus members and range from topically oriented research briefs to authoritative research guides that provide in-depth, authoritative analyses of trends and events.
- *Events*. Experts also participate in a variety of events, including roundtables, webcasts, and summits. Focus events are built around expert speakers and provide attendees with an opportunity to personally interact with experts.

Whether it's Q&A, research, or events, you can personalize all the expertise on Focus by following specific topics and experts. Focus is also easy to use and freely available to anyone who wants help in making better business decisions.

AroundMe (www.aroundmeapp.com). AroundMe allows you to quickly find out information about your surroundings, including a quick listing for categories of businesses such as banks/ATMs, bars, coffee shops, gas stations, hospitals, movie theaters, and more. If you're in an unfamiliar city or an area where you need to find a business quickly, AroundMe is invaluable for getting you oriented to your surroundings quickly.

Aroundme is available on iTunes for iPhones, iPod touch, and iPad in several languages and from the Android Market for Androids.

CONTROLLING COMMUNICATIONS

◆ ◆ ◆

Social media is the new wave of selling. Make sure you're using every technology option to your advantage.

Clearly, what you say, how you say it, and when you say it are vitally important in communications with prospects throughout the sales cycle. This applies to voice mails and e-mails, marketing collaterals, websites, LinkedIn profiles (corporate and personal), Facebook, YouTube, Twitter, Google+, webinars, Vimeo, Flickr, Tagged (www.tagged.com), MySpace, MyLife (www.mylife.com), Meetup (www.meetup.com), blogs, and any other ways you communicate with your prospects and the general public in writing or verbally.

Depending on the size of your company, you may not have much direct control over the communications on your website and marketing collaterals. However, it is incumbent on you to bring negative client comments back into your marketing organization for evaluation and possible changes when the collaterals or website is refreshed. Without that feedback, your company may continue to use a poorly designed website and collaterals that don't support your sales efforts as they should.

What you do have complete control over is your personal communications: voice mails, e-mails, publicly available information and profiles about you, and texting. To participate in this highly connected business world, you must have a LinkedIn profile for yourself, and if there isn't a company-developed profile that is maintained centrally, you may be able to set one up that serves that purpose for you and your prospects.

CONTROL THE SOCIAL MEDIA MADNESS

HootSuite (www.hootsuite.com) is by far the best tool to manage your social media empire, find leads, and keep up on trends.

HootSuite is a social media management system that lets businesses and organizations collaboratively execute campaigns across multiple social networks from one secure web-based dashboard. Launch marketing campaigns, identify and grow audiences, and distribute targeted messages by using HootSuite's unique social media dashboard. Streamline team workflow with scheduling and assignment tools and reach audiences with geotargeting functionality. Invite multiple collaborators to manage social profiles securely and provide custom reports by using the comprehensive social analytics tools for measurement.

Key social network integrations include Facebook, Twitter, LinkedIn, and Google+ Pages, plus a suite of social content apps for YouTube, Flickr, Tumblr, and more.

Murphy's Law Web

We have all heard the horror stories about people posting pictures or rants that get them fired or never hired in the first place. In the age of the Internet, you are only a Google search away from your blog post rant, YouTube videos of college pranks, spring break bikini photos, and much more. It's one thing to make poor choices and act immaturely when we're young. It's quite another when it's captured and posted without your knowledge online a decade later.

You will never know for sure if a prospect or customer has searched for you within the multitude of social media sites, but you should assume that prospects do this. According to a 2009 Career-Builder survey,[1] as many as 45 percent of prospective employers are using social networks to look at job applicants' private lives, and that number is increasing every day. Interestingly, they check Facebook more than LinkedIn; that's why you want to make sure your Facebook page doesn't include damaging or unsavory information about you. If you can't make an objective judgment call on what's acceptable, ask your parents, a trusted friend, or a sibling to look at your page or profile to give you constructive feedback.

A motivated company considering a big-dollar investment in your consultant services or evaluating your company as a business partner will vet you as thoroughly as any politician is vetted for public office. The plethora of free public information available on you is staggering (in addition to what is available with payment), and you cannot afford to bad-mouth your company, clients, spouse, or competitor anywhere because it is guaranteed to come back and bite you.

When Mr. Target budgets money to have you and your company solve his pain, he must find you to be professional and above reproach in every aspect of your online exposure, both business and personal.

Bottom line: Selling has changed over the last five years; you need to be up to date with all the media and leverage them to your selling advantage. You need to get inside your prospect's circle and make your pitch count.

◆◆◆

Balance is the key when you're in sales.

CHAPTER 7

◆◆◆

BREACHING THE FORTRESS

We don't know where our first impressions come from or precisely what they mean, so we don't always appreciate their fragility.

MALCOLM GLADWELL

How many times have you received a hand-addressed envelope except from your relatives? That's exactly the reason this process works: people are intrigued by the novelty and will open your letter first. We live in a society that is overloaded with information, and it gets worse every year. The average person receives thousands of messages from e-mail, television, texting, mail, fax, phone, and in-person conversations. We sort our lives over the wastepaper basket and the recycling bin and by hitting the delete button for our e-mails and voice mails.

If you want to be successful in sales, it's critical to do the little things that will add up quickly to your benefit and set you apart from your peers and competitors. Start with the personal touch in your opening letter; it will make all the difference in the world.

I've been told countless times how impressed my prospects were by my approach and that they enjoyed reading my letters.

This entire chapter is focused on your approach to the prospect and how to use a variety of communication tools to get inside the business to the target decision maker who can sign the purchase order for your product, service, or solution.

APPROACH LETTERS

The very first impression your prospect forms of you comes from your approach letter. As we'll discuss, you'll use a general template, but don't make it a form letter: each prospect must feel you are thoroughly knowledgeable about his company and his pain and are able to help.

Format your letters as you were taught in Business 101 or in typing/keyboard/computer class.

By the way, there is no substitute for this first step. This is not e-mail. Write a formal letter, print it out, sign it, put a stamp on it, and mail it.

On the next pages are my template and three real examples from clients of mine, with details changed to protect their competitive edge.

Figure 7.1 shows the approach letter template you should use.

sales S ense™
Solutions, Inc.

Sales Sense Letter Framework

Dear: _____

▶ **Question or grabber:**

What if _____, what would this mean to your business?
{you could achieve a 10 to 30 % increase in revenue or reduction in time or cost}

▶ **Result of using our services:**

Our clients have saved over _____ and _____ to the bottom line.
{10 to 20 % in time using our system, resulting in less turnover}   {adding 10 to 20 % in revenue}

Three critical areas separate_____ from all others:
{our company/product/service}

▶ **Unique Selling Proposition:**

- Unique value proposition:
    - ✓ I help (target) solve (key need/want) by (what you do).
- Why people buy from you:
    - ✓ Our best customers tell us they like _____.
- If you went out of business today, what customers would miss most:
    - ✓ and our _____ is why they keep buying from us year over year.

▶ **Testimonial from client, if you have approval:**

<name> of <company> wrote a letter to our president recently that mentioned: _____.
I will call you _____ to introduce myself and learn more about your business and (key need/want).

Respectfully,

<your name>
<company>
<contact information>

By taking a few moments to speak with me, you will receive _____ or the extension of an offer.

©2012 Sales Sense Solutions, Inc.

FIGURE 7.1

J. D. Brown

Date

Mr. Prospect
Address 1
Address 2
City, State, Zip

Dear _____:

Are you frustrated with your current document management solution?

Results from our clients:

- 30–50 percent increase in productivity
- Savings of over $15,000 on average
- Reduction in errors
- Work space increased

Document organization, sharing, and security are important to any organization, be it a small company or a large organization. [Your company name] is offering a simple, affordable, robust solution to electronic document management that enables you to share documents residing on your own server with other users. The documents are secure behind authorization algorithms and an encrypted database table data.

[Your company name] offers the ideal solution for document storage and preservation: [product name]. A medium that will last for at least 500 years, is resistant to water, fire, and other physical damage, and can be accessed either digitally or optically.

Rather than keeping it in-house, take a look at us and the benefits; listen to what our clients are saying:

"I'll note that [product name] *has a great advantage over microfilm as well: the lack of any need for highly controlled storage environments to ensure preservation."*

JV, New York

I will call you on [date] to introduce myself and learn more about your business and help you achieve your goals.

Respectfully,

Sales Winner
VP Technology
Company Name
Address
Phone: (555) 555 4334 Ext. 15
Cell: (555) 555 6047
Fax: (555) 555 4336
www.company.com

Date

Mr. Samuel Prospect
XYZ Inc.
1 Market Drive
Commerce, NY 11111

Hello, Sam:

One question: Would your business grow if you could deliver the core message of your company in a clear, concise manner day and night to prospects, wherever they are?

In every supply chain there are companies that need to tell their story to traditional as well as new markets. Our clients deliver that message in a more consistent manner by using our expertise in video and multimedia production. To note a few:

Adobe Homes–Chodak–Oldie Foods–Practif–Guard Scaling Networks–Peterson Health–XYZ Technologies–Auction Contact NA–Sales Corp.

"Our whole objective was to come across with a very concise, precise, classy presentation of substance, and when I first saw the video, I was blown away."

I will call you at 9:50 a.m. Thursday February 4 to learn more about your marketing efforts, introduce myself, and set an appointment.

Thank you.

Andrew Sales
New Business Development
555-555-6674
LinkedIn Profile

Date

Mr. Prospect
Address
City, State, Zip

Dear Mr. Prospect:

Frustrated with your rising vehicle costs? What if [Company Name] could save 15–20 percent on how much it costs to operate your vehicles? What would this mean to your business?

Results of using our services:

- Proven fleet management program
- Dedicated to controlling expenses by 20 percent
- Generated positive cash flow.

There are three critical areas that separate [Company Name] from all others:

- Personal attention to companies with between 10 and 200 vehicles
- Total transportation provider that focuses on lowering costs and helping increase image, reliability, and safety for its drivers.
- From acquisition to disposal we focus on every outgoing penny associated with each and every vehicle.

Testimonial from satisfied client:
"My local account manager has lowered our overall fleet costs by helping me proactively manage our fleet. I spend very little time worrying or thinking about our fleet anymore. I feel like we are in good hands and being well taken care of."

Bottom line: we solve cash flow management problems by providing strategic funding options. I will call you on Thursday October 7 at 9:00 a.m. I look forward to learning more about your business and helping you achieve your goals.

Respectfully,

James

James Sales
New Business Development
555-555-2620

Check Your Work

One major point to remember when you write anything: spell check, spell check, *spell check.*

Although some people (prospects, clients, managers) aren't picky about grammar and spelling, many are. You could ruin your first impression without ever shaking the prospect's hand. Make sure that you are spelling Mr. Target's name properly, that you spell all the words correctly, and that you're using correct grammar.

The spell check is only as good as the human at the keyboard, so be sure to read your message carefully to make sure all the right words are there and are spelled correctly. One trick writers and editors use is to read the message backward, from the end to the beginning, to spot missing and misspelled words. If English is not your first language, ask someone who will be objective to read the first draft of your approach messages and suggest constructive changes.

If you are one of the millions of people confused by *you're* and *your* or by *they're, their,* and *there,* do not use the contraction but spell out the words. If in doubt, look them up in an online dictionary such as Merriam-Webster.com, Dictionary.com, or TheFreeDictionary.com and create a cheat sheet to help you in this area.

APPROACH E-MAIL

In your approach e-mail, you need to demonstrate to the prospect that you understand her problems (pain) and her company sufficiently to provide the company with compelling value and/or a cure for its pain.

Make the body of the e-mail easy to read:
- Write in short paragraphs; even a single sentence per paragraph works.
- Your total message should be three to five lines at a maximum.
- Use the company and industry acronyms if you know what they mean and can use them correctly.
- Name-drop if the person whose name you're dropping approves.

Keep your words short and succinct; you may have a Harvard vocabulary, but this isn't the time to show it off.

Include white space and use a business font such as Times New Roman, Helvetica, or Arial (at least a 12-point font is good).

Spell check and spell check again; get someone else to read it for you if necessary.

Also check the readability scores in Word or Outlook (the steps to take to set this up in the 2007 suite are given below).

Readability Statistics

Follow this sequence:

1. Click the Microsoft Office button and then click Word Options.
2. Click Proofing.
3. Make sure "Check grammar with spelling" is selected.
4. Under "When correcting grammar in Word," select the "Show readability statistics" check box.

After this feature is enabled, open an e-mail and check your spelling. When Word finishes checking the spelling and grammar, it displays information about the reading level of the document. The readability tests are shown in the lower third of the dialog box, and the rating is based on the average number of syllables per word and the number of words per sentence.

Here is a summary that is easy to remember:

- *Flesch Reading Ease.* You want higher numbers; 60 to 70 is great.
- *Flesch-Kincaid Grade Level.* You want lower numbers; stay at 9 or below.

Just as important as your voice and your personal image is your e-mail image: the content and the timing of your message. There are definite advantages and disadvantages to consider when contacting your prospect by e-mail to set up the first appointment, as shown in the chart on the next page.

Advantages to Sending E-mail Appointment Requests	Disadvantages of Sending E-mail Appointment Requests
Quicker to send e-mails than to make phone calls	Not as personal a way to contact an important prospect; no way to react instantly and be persuasive
Less intimidating or frightening than making phone calls	Easy for prospect to delete message and dismiss you without giving you a shot
Avoids gatekeepers in some instances	The prospect will scan, open, and read when she has time; may not fit your time frame
Compose and send on your own time frame: time to calmly craft your message exactly as you want it	Golden opportunity for making mistakes in a written message (spelling, assumptions, etc.)

SUBJECT LINES

Think about the deluge of items in your company e-mail in-box and the way you decide which ones to open. Personal friends, family members, your boss, and business colleagues—those are the easy ones. What entices you to open an unsolicited e-mail or one from an unknown sender? There are a number of ways to improve your chances of having your e-mail reach Ms. Target (nimbly avoiding firewalls and spam filters) and then get opened.

As you might expect, there are different schools of thought about how to write a subject line that has the greatest open rate. You may need to do some testing and use a blend of the following suggestions to suit your sales environment and the prospects you target.

An e-mail message has roughly a one- to three-second window during which the recipient decides what to do with it:

1. Open it now
2. Delete it now
3. Forward it now
4. Hold it for later

Writing for Microsoft, Sally McGhee of McGhee Productivity Solutions[1] says that on average executives receive 100 e-mail messages each day and that it takes roughly one hour of uninterrupted time to scan through them to determine which of the four dispositions each one will receive. That's about 1.6 seconds for scanning the subject and sender and then deciding what to do with the e-mail.

The takeaway message is to write your e-mail subject line carefully, commanding the recipient's maximum level of interest.

To improve your chances, follow these points with every e-mail subject line, not just in appointment approach e-mails:

- The subject line should be no more than 50 characters maximum.
- Make your grabber prominent in the subject line.
- Always use the same e-mail account: your professional one, not a friends-only one such as gotbeer247365@XYZ.com or iheartfluffyunicorns2@XYZ.com.
- Avoid spam filters by leaving out punctuation.
- Don't type words in all caps.
- Don't use color fonts or attach pictures or logos as images; spam filters love these too.
- Words such as *free, credit, offer,* and *act now* trigger spam filters, so leave them out.
- Try not to include attachments.

There are a number of words that HubSpot's Webinar on the Science of Email Marketing,[2] researched and presented by Dan Zarrella, show will get your e-mail opened more frequently. Find ways to use them in your subject line. The same webinar lists a number of words that are overused and much abused in e-mail marketing, and so you would do well to avoid them in the subject line of any e-mails you send.

Use These Words	Don't Use These Words
posts	confirms
jobs	features
survey	upgrade
week's	magic
e-newsletter	raffle
issue	requested
digest	rewards
bulletin	Christ
edition	free
giveaway	15.00 percent
tips	discount
video	savings
news	offer
monthly	
headlines	
latest	
updates	

Using these guidelines, here are sample subject lines that should get Ms. Target's attention. I advocate brief, teaser-type subject lines that require the prospect to open the message to decide what to do with it. Here are some examples of these kinds of subject lines:

- Can we talk Wednesday at 2:10?
- Brief survey about . . .
- Video newsletter . . .
- A quick question about . . .
- A thought about . . .
- Your thoughts on . . . ?

Again, you probably will have to tinker with your subject line writing and test what works best for your industry and your prospects.

My personal favorite is "As promised." I like this one because I'm building trust in the relationship and proving that they can count on me.

Try writing a few versions of your approach e-mail subject line to find some that work for you.

ALL ABOUT YOUR OPENING STATEMENT

In his book *Blink*, Malcolm Gladwell introduces the concept of rapid cognition. Gladwell defines rapid cognition as "the kind of thinking that happens in the blink of an eye. When you meet someone for the first time, or walk into a house you are thinking of buying, or read the first few sentences of a book, your mind takes about two seconds to jump to a series of conclusions. . . . Those instant conclusions that we reach are really powerful and really important and, occasionally, really good."[3]

Besides actually sitting down and doing it, nothing is more important in targeting and prospecting than developing an attention-getting opening statement that stops the target in his or her tracks. You may think of the opening statement as primarily for voice mail and live conversations, but you need a well-refined opening statement for e-mails and mailed approach letters too.

According to Gladwell, the first impression is formed within the first two seconds. Other studies have shown that in person, online, or over the phone, your window of opportunity to grab someone's attention slams shut in 10 seconds or less. This means you must make every word, syllable, and pause in your leadoff statement count, as though you were shooting bullets at point-blank range. Your opening statement must be compelling.

If you do not believe in taking the time to build a rock-solid opening statement or are not willing to do it, you are wasting your time, your company's time, and the client's time. Perhaps this is the time when you should decide you would be better off in a different line of work.

The good news is that you can write the opening statement in draft form and then practice and refine it repeatedly *before* you start your revamped SMART Prospecting process. I've created some guidelines and tips to help you develop the basic opening statement. I've also given you some samples that you may be able to use as templates for your particular industry and prospects.

A strong attention-getting opening statement delivered confidently and flawlessly will put your sales process on the fast track in situations in which your competitor's inability to capture the client's interest in the way I'm showing you will put you in first place every time. You are not the only one attempting to snag this company or this target decision maker, and so you have to be different, compelling, and prepared.

OPENING STATEMENT MASTERY

As in any great spy movie, your prospecting mission here, should you choose to accept it, is to create enthusiasm and immediate interest in your decision-making target's mind, paving the way for the first appointment and further selling dialogue. You want to capture prospects' undivided attention so effectively that they are eager to learn more from you.

Start with Benefits

Step inside the target's mindset so that you can understand the benefits of your product, service, or solution from his perspective. If you put the "what's in it for me" (WIIFM) hook up front, you will have his attention, guaranteed. By the way, this works for business-to-consumer selling as well as it does for business-to-business sales. This is a good time to leaf back to Chapter 1, "How Does a Prospect Think?" and review the work you did on identifying behavior and learning styles for your prospect and yourself.

What's New?

One of the best ways to grab a prospect's attention is to include a reference to her company's recent press mentions or latest activities in your message. It's easy to have current topical information about the company delivered automatically to your computer whenever events or mentions occur by using Google Alerts.

Google Alerts are e-mail updates of the latest relevant Google results (web, news, and more) that are based on your choice of query or topic. In Google Alerts, enter the topic (in this case the company) you wish to monitor and then click Preview to see the types of results you'll receive. Some other handy uses of Google Alerts include the following:

- Monitoring a developing news story
- Keeping current on a competitor or industry
- Getting the latest on a celebrity or event
- Keeping tabs on your favorite sports teams[4]

Simplify Your Approach

Speaking in plain English, describe what you are selling as simply as possible: the *Reader's Digest* ninth-grade reading-level[5] version. Stay away from acronyms, jargon, techno-speak, and the lofty words written in brochures by the marketing department. When you're writing, say it out loud to your spouse, your grandmother, and your 15-year-old cousin. If it's understandable to them—meaning that they can tell you what you're selling in their own words—you can use it in the opening statement. If they don't get it, go back to the drawing board until it's clear to anyone not familiar with your business.

What you say in your message is also crucial. Here it's time for the KISS strategy: *keep it* short and sweet. Keep the focus on the recipient and the immediate benefit to his business: do not talk about you, your company, or your great solution. Save that for later in the sales cycle.

◆◆◆

Keep your client or prospect informed at each step so that
he never feels left out.

MORE GOOD WORDS TO USE

There are many powerful words from which to create the opening statement. You'll find the same 13 words used repeatedly in marketing and advertising, because they cause an automatic, visceral reaction in most people (probably because they directly address our inner FUD: fear, uncertainty, and doubt). If possible, weave a couple of these top 13 words into your statement:

- You
- Money
- Save
- New
- Easy
- Love
- Discover
- Discovery
- Results
- Health
- Proven
- Guarantee
- Free

In addition, the words listed below will help you create a powerful opening statement. Again, keep the behavior and learning models in mind as you select the words that will have the greatest impact on your prospect:

- Expand, maximize, boost, increase, grow, focus (followed by productivity, your customer base, sales, customer loyalty, or other key business factors)
- Reduce, minimize, eliminate, decrease (followed by specific points of pain, such as expenses, customer service complaints, and distractions)
- Benefit
- Retain, conserve, save
- Particular, exclusive, exclusively, specifically

- Entirely, completely, fully, wholly
- Accumulate, add, acquire, collect, build
- Stop, avoid, prevent
- Now, priority, urgent, immediate, instantly

AVOID WORN-OUT PHRASES

Although the phrases and statements listed next may be relevant and appropriately friendly later in the sales cycle with your prospects, they are akin to asking, "What's your sign?" to open a conversation in a bar with a person you find attractive. Don't use them in your opening statement either on the phone or in an e-mail because they turn people off instantly.

These phrases, statements, and clichés do not command attention or **increase** a prospect's receptivity. Worse, they detract from your strong opening statement, rob you of your personal power, and stop the prospect from listening to or reading what you're saying:

- I'd like to understand more about [the target business] to see . . .
- How are you today?
- Is now a good time for us to talk?
- [Our company] is the top provider of . . .
- We are already working with [competitors of target].
- I'd like to see if there are some ways we might work together.
- Did I catch you at a bad time?

Don't Forget FUD

Think about what your prospect's emotional response and personal benefits are, not just the tangible and quantitative advantages of using your products or services. Will the prospects have less stress? Do they pine for fewer daily headaches and fire drills? Will their value and stature rise in the company if they solve a tough issue or improve profits? Every person on this earth experiences fear, uncertainty, and doubt (affectionately shortened to FUD in marketing and sales circles) in her or his professional and private life. How are your products or services addressing these factors?

The first acknowledged intentional use of FUD was to discredit IBM's competitors with misinformation or half-truths,[6] but that's not the FUD we mean here. We're referring to the more generalized use: understanding and playing to a person's emotional reactions can be a potent sales tool. FUD examples include the questions people ask themselves all the time, often in the middle of the night, such as the following:

- Will I get promoted if it saves us money?
- Could this get me fired if it backfires?
- Do I have the authority to do this?
- Can we afford it?
- Will it work?
- How do I know this person is telling me the truth?
- Will this hurt?
- Can I see it working somewhere else?
- How can this benefit me?
- Does this person like me?
- Can I do this?
- What if I fail?

These are all FUD-fueled (nearly always unspoken) questions and concerns that refer directly to the person rather than to the company.

Turn to the Opening Statement Template in Appendix B. You'll create your entire approach message in just a little while. For now, just capture all the important information.

Obviously, your overall e-mail image includes the subject line, the salutation, the impeccably written message body, and a strong close. Keep everything about the approach e-mail professional and business-like. You don't need exclamation marks, humorous asides, or fancy electronic stationery to weasel your way into the prospect's awareness. If anything, these distractions could reflect negatively on your professionalism and spell doom for your approach.

Electronic stationery is available in most e-mail programs. If the choice whether to use it yours, don't use patterned stationery with clients; reserve it for your family and friends. Stick with the plain white background of standard e-mails and you can't go wrong.

Signature Blocks

Among the subtlest ways to create a professional image in this electronic age of communications is to create a signature block, including the company logo, contact information, and your title. You set this up once in your e-mail program and then can include it or not, depending on the message and its intended recipient. In addition to providing you with a more professional image, it is a big time-saver in that you do not have to retype your personal information a hundred times a day.

Here are two examples of signature blocks, although yours would not have a border around them on your e-mails.

Samantha Sales, Account Executive
WidgetWorld Enterprises, Inc.
Direct line: 555-522-5555
E-mail: sam.sales@widget.com

To Your SALes Success!

Mike

585-704-6453
www.SalesSenseSolutions.com

Some e-mail programs allow you to set up several signature blocks so that your spouse and grandmother don't get the business signature block and your prospects don't get the cute personal signature. You select whichever signature block you want at the bottom of each e-mail.

Whether you use a signature block or not, always include your contact information to facilitate easier communication. For some sales professionals, such as those in real estate, including your photograph and/or your company logo can give you added credibility and recognition, particularly if you are new to the industry, territory, or company. Make sure to use a recent professionally taken picture, not your yearbook picture from 20 years ago or a great snapshot from your vacation.

E-MAIL TIMING

This one can be tricky. Try to schedule your message to arrive on a Tuesday, Wednesday, or Thursday, because Mondays are busy with staff meetings and putting out fires that occurred over the weekend. Fridays aren't much better. By Friday, your prospect is already on the golf course, at least mentally, or is so tired of sales pitches and calls that you may not get through the clutter even if you craft an Academy Award–winning statement.

Having your message arrive after hours (or in the early hours of the morning, say, 6:30 a.m.) is a good technique, especially since CEOs and other C-level position holders are typically still at the office well beyond 5:00 p.m. and usually get in before 9:00 a.m., and so there is a chance that they'll look at it right away. Most e-mail programs will let you schedule when a message will be sent, and so you don't have to be sitting at your desk at the exact time you want the message to go out.

Avoid starting a big pitch to a key prospect just before the December holidays (as in the day before; there's plenty of opportunity earlier in December, so don't write off the entire month as a waste of time for prospecting) or certain other key dates. If the gatekeeper or the prospect mentions that he is going on vacation or an overseas business trip the next day, put a reminder in your calendar to approach him two or three days after he is back in the office.

If the prospect is involved with financial matters—month, quarter, half-year, or year-end closes—or gets very busy during tax season, postpone your approach until she can focus on your solutions without worrying about what requires her attention in her regular work. Do the same thing with industry trade shows, road shows, conferences, and conventions: if your prospect is heavily involved as a keynote speaker, announcing new products, or doing any number of other show-related activities, leave her alone until after the dust settles.

This means you need to know enough about the industry the prospect is in and what his outward-focused and customer-focused activities are that you know to approach him when there is the best chance that he will be receptive and able to talk with you. Do your research to learn personal, company, and industry schedules. Most company websites have an event section, or you can look through the company's recent press releases to see if it has announced a user group convention or upcoming participation in an industry event.

VOICE MAIL AND LIVE MESSAGES

We have all become accustomed to leaving and returning voice mails, and so it is often a surprise when a live person picks up the phone and we have to recompose our words on the fly and have an interactive conversation. In creating a script for your SMART Prospecting calls, leave sufficient flexibility so that you can switch from voice mail mode to live mode without getting flustered and sounding unprepared.

We've already worked on your opening statement a bit, but we need to create the entire conversation so that it flows well as an interactive dialogue *or* as a one-sided voice mail. Switching from voice mail mode to live mode isn't much different from using a recipe to make lasagna or brownies. When you realize you don't have one ingredient, you quickly substitute another.

SACRED RULES OF ALL APPROACH CALLS

Make sure to follow these seven rules:

1. *Be prepared.* Do your research on the company and the prospect you're calling. If there is any recent news you can leverage, such as an interview, a new stock offering, a reorganization, or a new product, weave that information into the call. In all cases, keep it professional. If her daughter just got married, leave that out.

2. *Exception:* If he hit a hole in one over the weekend, she won a regional tennis match, or he just completed a triathlon, it's all right to incorporate that information if you can do it without sounding like you're kissing up.

3. *Leave your phone number twice:* once at the beginning of the call with your name and again at the end of the call. Speak slowly and pause so that the person has a chance to write down your contact information.

4. *Work from a script.* Don't try to do this on the fly or you'll crash every time. Have script variants at hand for different scenarios: talking with a gatekeeper, an unexpected live pickup, a voice mail message, and so on.

5. *Honor your commitments.* If you say you'll call at 9:52 a.m., you'd better make the follow-up call at that time.

6. *Don't embellish* your successes, referral names, or percentage gains. Maintain your integrity. Find something creative to say if you don't have the numbers or customers to back you up. Write this into your script.

7. *Don't overpromise.* Commit only to what you can honestly and truthfully deliver. You won't get anywhere by being liked for your promises; you are only as good as your deliveries.

8. *Be concise.* Keep your call to about 45 seconds and your e-mail message to five lines or fewer.

♦♦♦

You don't know everything, so don't be afraid to tell your prospect that you don't know something. Then follow up as quickly as possible with the answer.

Sales Pro Tips

Take note of the following tips:

- Never call on a Monday, when there are staff meetings and every possible problem in the world has landed on your prospect's desk. Mondays are for closing.

- The best time to call is on Thursday between 7:30 a.m. and 1:00 p.m.; it's also best not to call on Friday afternoon. Of course, I always recommend calling before 9:00 a.m. and after 5:00 p.m. to avoid the gatekeeper entirely and speak directly with the decision maker, who is definitely working more than a nine-to-five schedule. My personal favorite time to call is about 6:00 p.m. or a bit later in the evening.
- In speaking with the decision maker on this call—or any call— do not start with any variation on the phrase "I'm just following up on [packet or message]" as it gives the decision maker the option to stall you, get rid of you, or toss objections in your path. You're begging to be put off or sidelined. Instead, assume an upbeat tone, smile, stand up, and start with a positive approach. Take control of the call and your SMART Prospecting process from the start. Assume that prospects are eager to meet with you because you have the best cure for their work pain since sliced bread.

◆◆◆

After each sales call, write down what went right and what went wrong so that you get better with every call.

SCRIPT MASTERY WORKSHOP

Now let's work on creating the scripts you will use for your calls and e-mails. We will go through them in the order in which you are most often going to use them.

Call Script: Find the Decision Maker

If you don't know the name of the decision maker, you'll first speak with a gatekeeper, usually an administrative assistant or receptionist: someone whose job it is to field calls from vendors and sales professionals and make them go away. Make this call when you are ready to start the sales process with this client and you're preparing the approach letter. Remember that you want your voice to come across as excited, upbeat, and happy without sounding goofy.

Hello, this is [Your Name] from [Your Company].
Could you please direct me to the person who makes decisions about _____?
What is the best time to reach him?
Could you tell me her e-mail address?
Does he have a direct phone number?

Tips

Follow these tips:

- Always try to get something from a conversation with a gatekeeper. Obtain business intelligence on every call.
- Make sure to get the proper spelling of the prospect's name, along with the title, the e-mail address, and a complete telephone number.
- If the person you're trying to reach has a gender-neutral first name such as Sam, Pat, Devon, or Taylor or a name from a different culture that you aren't sure about, ask the gatekeeper whether the person is a woman or a man. Better to ask the question up front than to be embarrassed by guessing and addressing your correspondence incorrectly.
- If the gatekeeper/administrator/receptionist identifies himself or herself by name, make a note of that too. Remembering that person's name when you call again will earn you a bagful of brownie points and, quite likely, better treatment.
- Always conclude live calls and voice mails with a sincere "Thank you very much." Keep it short and sweet.

If the decision maker picks up when you call, introduce yourself briefly and then tell her you will be sending out a letter summarizing your services.

◆◆◆

Study and learn your prospect's buying process and adapt to that, *not* to your sales process.

Call Script: Decision Maker Identified, Voice Mail Option

Hello, [gatekeeper's name if you know it]. This is [your name] from [your company].

     Is _____ in?

     Gatekeeper: *No. May I put you through to his voice mail?*

Instead of answering the question directly, ask your own question to get some additional information: the correct spelling of names, full titles, e-mail addresses, best times to catch the decision maker, and whether this is the person you should be calling or if there is someone else who might be better qualified and authorized to speak with you. At this point, don't leave a voice mail unless you have done some additional fact-finding and are thoroughly prepared with your voice mail scripts and agenda.

More than likely, you won't get an opportunity to speak with the decision maker on the first call unless the gatekeeper is new or just filling in. What you should have by the end of the call with the gatekeeper is the name of the decision maker, the name of the gatekeeper, how to spell both names, the decision maker's title, an e-mail address, and the best times to reach the decision maker. This is golden information that should go immediately into your CRM system.

SCRIPT EXAMPLES AND CREATION

We'll go through examples for each type of script: a bad example (courtesy of the Sales Clown) and a revised good example used by a sales pro; then you can write one of your own. There is also a live call example that the sales pro made.

Sales Clown Sample Voice Mail 1

Hey, uh [Pat]. How're ya today? Ah, um, Sam Clownson of XYZ here. I'm calling to offer you the best deal on SEO services you will ever see! Are you familiar with SEO? Are you currently using SEO on your, um [papers rustling loudly, loud talking in background] website, right?

Would you be interested in [shoves some popcorn into his mouth) learning more about our SEO services? We are doing SEO to most of your competitors, including Acme Industrial of Topeka, and I'm sure you don't want them to get ahead of you in the market, right? [ha ha] If you get a chance, shoot me a call back so we can get together, right? Have a great day!

Identify the mistakes that Sales Clown Sam made in this call. Think about the areas in which he made mistakes:

- Addressing the prospect respectfully
- Opening
- Identifying himself
- Grabber
- Noise
- Preparedness
- Understanding the prospect's business
- Mumbling or eating on the phone
- Closed-ended question
- Name-dropping/boasting
- Inappropriate joking
- Informal speech
- Trite clichéd phrases
- No phone number left
- Didn't repeat name

Sales Pro Sample Voice Mail 1

Good morning, Mr. Patton. This is Wendy Winner of XYZ at 888-888-8888. I just read the interview you did with Biz Journal *where you* mentioned your 2012 objective to generate more leads through social media. I've helped four other [same industry] companies in the past year to develop complete social media campaigns that are adding 10 to 15 qualified prospects to their databases per month.

I will be in Dallas next week, and we could meet for 30 minutes so I can explain further. I will call you tomorrow at 9:45 a.m. so we can set something up. Again, this is Wendy Winner of XYZ at 888-888-8888. Have a great day.

What did Sales Pro Wendy do well in this call?

Your Turn

Write a voice mail example you could use with a prospect today.

SALES PRO LIVE CALL 1

Good afternoon, Mr. Patton.

This is Wendy Winner of XYZ in Atlanta. I was just reading your interview with Biz Journal where you mentioned your 2012 objective to generate more leads through social media.

I'm calling because I've helped four other industrial consultant companies in the past year develop complete social media campaigns that are adding 10 to 15 qualified prospects to their databases per month.

I will be in Dallas next week if you could meet for 30 minutes so I can explain further.

Would Tuesday or Wednesday work better for you? Great!

What's better: morning or afternoon? Great!

Would 9:00 a.m. or 11:00 a.m. work with your schedule? All right. So we'll meet at 11:00 a.m., Wednesday, April 20.

Could I please have your e-mail so I can send you a reminder note for your calendar and a white paper we did recently on SEO opportunities for consultants? Thank you.

I'm looking forward to meeting with you. Have a great day!

Using the same scenario, here are the e-mails Sales Clown Sam and Sales Pro Wendy sent to this prospect.

Sales Clown E-mail 1

Subject: XYZ can help you grow!

Hi Pat,

Our business, XYZ, is the largest SEO operation in the United States. I believe every company—including ones like yours—needs SEO services these days to generate more leads through social media. There's never been a better time to get on the social media bandwagon, and we are just the company to help you get there! We'll even discount your first 12 months with us to make it more attractive.

Most of my clients have seen their leads go up at least 50 percent because of our services, including your good friends at Acme Industrial, Triplex Services, Bastion and Grable Supply, Calabreese Corporation, Martson Enterprises, Denver Affiliates, and many others.

Anyway, I can squeeze you in next week so you can see how great SEO can be for your business.

Hey, call at your earliest convenience so we can get together while I'm in Dallas.

Sam Clownson

Identify the mistakes Sales Clown Sam made in his e-mail approach.

Sales Pro E-mail 1

Subject: Ideas to meet or exceed 2012 objectives

Hi, Mr. Patton,

I just read your interview in the Biz Journal where you mentioned your 2012 objective to generate more leads through social media.

I've personally helped four other industrial consultant companies in the past year to develop complete social media campaigns that are adding 10 to 15 qualified prospects to their databases per month.

I will be in Dallas next week if you can meet for 30 minutes so I can explain further. I will call you tomorrow at 9:45 a.m. so we can set something up.

Best regards,

Wendy Winner, Sales Pro

XYZ World

(888) 888-8888

Wendy.winner@.com

Your Turn

Now it's your turn. Write an e-mail approach for one of your prospects that will have him calling you immediately.

◆◆◆

The right question at the right time nets you a new client.

The Close

I hate the whole idea of closing a person. Don't get me wrong: if someone asked whether I like the hunt or the kill better, I would have to say it's the kill.

I am a true sales hunter by definition. I love the hunt, and I love celebrating the kill/win. Maybe that's why I am successful at selling: I am always looking for a better way, always hunting for better ideas and strategies to achieve sales success faster.

I did not figure this out overnight; it took years of struggling to do that. The great news is that you're way ahead of the game: you believe in continuous development, and you've proved that you want to achieve more in life—and your sales career—by reading this book.

You *will* be successful; it takes time, knowledge, and confidence in yourself. I did it, and so I know you can do it too.

Are you ready to learn the trick to closing?

Here is the answer: The trick is in the opening, *not* in the close. Let me repeat: *it's in the opening*, not *in the close*. Ask yourself the following:

Were you on time?
Were you professional?
Were you prepared?
Were you engaging?
Did you have great questions to ask?

Did you follow up?
Did you take great notes?
Did you send a thank-you card?

If you did none of these things, no matter how hard you try, you will never close the deal.

If you did all these things, you can use the following tactic to close the sale.

My favorite technique is the *assumptive close*: it is by far my best tactic. Why, you ask? It follows the natural progression and flow of a call if done correctly, and at the end it just makes sense. You will need to master the following three critical steps to take before the close:

1. Have your agreement filled out before the call; there is nothing worse than watching a sales professional fumble around with paperwork and look like a rookie.
2. Be organized. Don't go in and wing it. Be completely prepared to capitalize on the opportunity to provide great value for your client.
3. Ask! Don't forget to ask for the close. That's the number one reason sales don't close: you forget to ask.

Here is exactly what I say at the end of a call:

Mr./Mrs. Prospect, I have enjoyed our meetings so far, and I look forward to building a long-lasting relationship with you. I want to confirm what we have discussed to this point and how my solution is the perfect fit for you and [challenge/problem].

Then you list the points clearly and convincingly.
Pause.
Is that how you understand it as well?
Pause.
Do you have any final questions for me?
Pause.

Great! Let's get started. All I need is your okay at the bottom of this document and I will get you started immediately.

Do *not* speak during this critical phase of the process. Wait for the prospect to pick up the pen and sign her name. (I have waited 30 minutes for this to happen; you can wait too.)

If you have had a strong opener and have done what you have said along the way, you will not need to close your client.

◆ ◆ ◆

Problems always equal more sales opportunities.

OBJECTION HANDLING: HEAD THEM OFF AT THE PASS

Heading them off at the pass is widely thought of as *the* military strategy in warfare.

I have come to the conclusion after tens of thousands of calls and making a ton of mistakes that it boils down to you as the sales professional understanding your opponent. If you fail to understand your opponent, you will not get the sale and will walk out of the appointment scratching your head as your competition has a party at your expense.

Here are the four critical components of a sale:

1. *Money.* Do they have the budget? Did you ask about this early in the process?
2. *Decision maker.* Do you really have the decision maker, not the person who thinks he's the decision maker?
3. *Time frame.* Have you asked the critical question of when she would like the service or solution completed by?
4. *Pain.* Are they in serious pain or just looking for a Band-Aid? Does your solution really matter to them, or are they just a bit itchy and doing some preliminary window-shopping?

Have you asked the prospect the following questions?

Money. Do you have a budget in mind for this solution?
Decision maker. Can you walk me through your decision-making
  process?
Time frame. When would you like the solution installed? Have
  you thought of a contingency plan?
Pain. What happens if you don't get this solution under way
  this year? Is this project contingent on the success of other
  projects?

You might be asking yourself, When is Krause going to help me handle objections? I just did. If you follow this sequence of questions and ask them at the right time to the right person, you will eliminate the need to use tactics to handle objections. Why? Because you will have headed them off at the pass.

For those of you who still do not get it or need more help because you have backed yourself in a corner (trust me, I've been there many, many times), consider the following:

- Remember, if you're not the cheapest, tell them up front. Why?
  To head them off at the pass.
- Remember, if you need senior executive sign-off, tell them up
  front. Why? To head them off at the pass.
- Remember, if you need 180 days to implement, tell them up
  front. Why? To head them off at the pass.
- Remember, if you're not solving their true pain, tell them up
  front. Why? To head them off at the pass.

THE FAMOUS FEEL, FELT, FOUND

Every salesperson starts with "I understand how you feel."

Empathize with your customer. Tell him that you understand how he feels and why he has raised his sales objection.

Other people just like you feel the same way.
Other customers just like you felt the same way you do, and they
    bought from me.
This is what others have found.

This feel, felt, found sequence literally makes me sick to my stomach. Why? Because the last sales representative did the same thing and has trained your prospect to expect that it's coming. You have to be unique, and here is how to do that:

Honestly, here is the best way, and it only took me my entire career to figure it out. Thanks to me, you now get a jump-start on your competition.

The key is to ask a question back.

Here's how:

The biggest objection: "You're too expensive." Your response should be "Compared to what?" Let the prospect tell you what she is comparing you with. Apples or oranges?

Any objection: Ask, "How do you mean that? Let the prospect tell you more because more than likely he is not telling you his true objection. You need to peel back the onion and get to the heart of the issue.

Any objection: Another question you should ask is "Why do you ask?" Again, let your prospect keep talking and get to the real issue behind his blustering with objections.

The key here is knowing your competition, having confidence in your solution, and asking the right questions up front. Why? To head them off at the pass.

◆ ◆ ◆

Great questions equal great relationships; questions are the
first step toward handling objections.

OBJECTION RESPONSES

Here's how to respond to a prospect's objections:

Not interested or the no budget objection. Focus your response to
this type of objection on the benefits your product or service
provides. Mention another customer who at first didn't have an
interest but after he saw a product demo realized that he really
needed the XYZ benefit your company provides and/or could
not afford not to forgo it.

Happy enough now: the don't rock the boat objection. If your prospect
is using someone or something else now, focus your response on
how your product or service complements the product or service
or alternative method she currently uses. Mention another customer who uses you along with the other product or service or
alternative method. This will get you in the door, and then you
can focus on unseating your competition.

Bad experience: the hate change objection. If the prospect has had
a bad experience with your company and/or your product or
service in the past, focus on how you've changed to address that
situation. If she has had a bad experience with a competitor,
point out your differences in that area.

The send literature brush-off objection. Come back with "Of course
I'm happy to, but I'm just curious [then ask an open-ended
question]." You should send literature when requested to do so,
but use the opportunity to find out more about what they do
now, what they would be most interested in seeing, and so forth.
This knowledge will allow you to send the right information
as well as create an open dialogue about their real interests
(and pain).

◆ ◆ ◆

Make sense out of the senseless.

Sixteen Strategies (and a Bonus) to Shorten the Sales Cycle

Here are 16 techniques you can use:

1. Send information before the appointment. This will allow the prospect to have time to digest your company's information and ask better questions when you meet face to face.
2. Set up a 10-minute conference call with your contact to set everyone's expectations for the meeting. Ask how they like to be presented to and cover any other necessary elements for a successful meeting, using PowerPoint presentations, brochures, interactive media, or printed copies.
3. Do research on every person who will be involved in the meeting by using LinkedIn and look for any common connection. Join the same groups the prospect belongs to if necessary.
4. Use Google Alerts; put your prospect in as an alert to keep you up to date with any breaking news.
5. Prepare for the meeting as though you were a doctor preparing for surgery. Read every page of the target company's website to understand their business, register for their newsletter, and follow them on Facebook and Twitter.
6. Print out all documents to bring to the first meeting and create a separate folder with the prospect's name on it.
7. Create an agenda for the meeting and make enough copies for all the attendees. Have the company's logo on the agenda.
8. Bring plenty of business cards and have them easily accessible. Make sure you look presentable and professional.
9. During the meeting, make sure to ask, "Can you walk me through the typical decision-making process, please?" This will clarify who the true decision maker is even if that person is not going to be present at the initial meeting.
10. Ask, "Have you thought of a budget for this project?" It helps clarify whether they have thought the project through or are just going through the motions with you and wasting your time.

11. Ask, "Have you thought of a plan B if this project does not work out or doesn't get funded?" This clarifies the extent to which they have thought it through and what their contingency plan is.

12. Ask, "What other solutions have you looked at?" This identifies who your competition is and whether the prospect is really just window-shopping and thinking of doing nothing.

13. Ask, "When would you like this project completed?" It clarifies whether your solution and their time frame are a fit and also helps create a sense of urgency.

14. Leave the meeting with next steps and action items clearly in place and the next event/meeting/call on all the decision makers' calendars.

15. Send out a pain letter: a summary sent out to all parties (decision makers, influencers, and implementers) who were at the meeting or not at the meeting. This sets up clear communications and an understanding of the meeting and smokes out any potential roadblocks.

16. Send out a handwritten thank-you note to each person at the meeting.

Here are some bonus tips:

- Come to the meeting prepared with the 10 key questions to ask the prospect.
- Arrive 10 minutes early.
- Dress appropriately and be well groomed.
- Ask about security in the building.
- Be friendly.
- Be respectful of the meeting time.
- Follow up fast and often.
- Reclarify all questions so that you all remain on the same page.
- Practice active listening.

- Look directly at the person who is speaking.
- Stop fidgeting, tapping, twitching, and engaging in any other nervous habits.
- Make sure your phone and/or PDA are put away, turned off, or silent.
- Take thorough notes.
- Always ask, "Is there anything else that I can provide you to help you make an informed decision?"

Create value at every meeting with your prospects and clients. Always close each meeting with the next steps clearly in place.

MORE EXAMPLES

Sales Clown Sample Voice Mail 2

Charlie, this is Sam Clownson, XYZ International. I met a gal from your company, uh, I think her name was Jackie—no, Janis—Fergus or something like that at a Digital Detroit networking event yesterday, and she said you were looking for a new PR firm to help your company's marketing. XYZ International—I'm sure you've heard of us—is mostly a telemarketing firm, but we are now getting into some PR and marketing too. Our goal is to increase our client list by 25 percent by the middle of next year with these new services.

Maybe you could give me a call so we can talk about how our services can help build your uh, er business. [Sam shifts the phone down below his chin so he's barely audible.]

Let's see when we can get together so we can boost your PR and marketing along with getting you into more inbound and outbound telephone sales. My number is 888-[mumble]-694.

Give Sam's latest voice mail a careful review and jot down the mistakes that will ensure that he never hears from his prospect.

Sales Pro Sample Voice Mail 2

Hi, Mr. Ryan. This is Wendy Winner with XYZ International, 555 [pause] 555 [pause] 2302. I met your marketing manager, Jackie Ferguson, yesterday, and she said your company was just beginning to look for a new PR firm to help your company's market presence.

I've done some research on your website, and I have several ideas that would improve your visibility and save you some money at the same time.

Using our services, our newest client just measured their awareness gain at 16 percent for the last six months. XYZ International blends PR with marketing and inbound/outbound telemarketing.

I'd like to meet with you as soon as it's convenient to go over my thoughts with you before you make a final decision. I'll call you tomorrow at 11:50 a.m. to set up our meeting. Again, this is Wendy Winner with XYZ International, 555 [pause] 555 [pause] 2302. Have a good day!

◆◆◆

Never be afraid to pick up the phone: you're selling to
a real person, not a computer.

Your Turn

Now it's your turn. Write a voice mail for one of your prospects that will have her on the phone right away.

Sales Pro Sample Live Call 2

Good afternoon, Mr. Ryan.

I'm Wendy Winner from XYZ International. I met Jackie Ferguson of your marketing department yesterday, and she mentioned you were looking for a new PR firm to help your company's market presence. She suggested I give you a call.

I've done some research on your company, and I have several ideas that I know would improve your visibility and save you money at the same time. Our newest client just measured their awareness gain at 16 percent for the last six months.

Our company combines classic PR with the latest marketing methods as well as inbound and outbound telemarketing.

I'd like to meet with you as soon as it's convenient to go over these ideas before you make a final decision.

Are you available Friday or next Tuesday? Great!

What's better: morning or afternoon? Great!

Would 2:00 p.m. or 4:00 p.m. work with your schedule? Wonderful. So we'll meet at 4:00 p.m., Friday, June 24.

Could I please have your e-mail so I can send you a reminder note for your calendar? Here's my personal cell number in case anything comes up: 555 [pause] 555 [pause] 2302. Thank you. Have a great day!

Sales Clown Sample E-mail 2

Dear Charlie,

I met Jackie Ferguson, Zane Killeen, Bob Wallins, Cal Mertz, and Kathy Brdlik at Digital Detroit yesterday. While we were talking, Jackie mentioned your company is looking for a new PR firm to help boost your market presence.

XYZ International is one of the largest inbound and outbound telemarketing firms in the country, and we are ramping up our public relations and marketing expertise at this time. Our best client just increased their marketing awareness at 16 percent for the last six months.

I'm certain we have the right services and products to help your company, and I'm so sure that I'd like to have you call a meeting with your marketing and PR people so I can show you what we have to offer.

I'm going to be in and out of the office most of the day, but I'll try to call you sometime tomorrow to set up a meeting. We have some great stuff for you!

Sam Clownson, S.C.

XYZ International

What did Sam the Sales Clown do poorly in his e-mail?

Sales Pro Sample E-mail 2

Mr. Ryan,

I met Jackie Ferguson of your marketing department yesterday, and she mentioned your company is looking for a new PR firm to help boost your market presence.

I've done some research on your company website, and I have several ideas that would improve your visibility and save you money at the same time.

In fact, one of our clients just measured their awareness gain at 16 percent for the last six months.

I'd like to meet with you as soon as it's convenient to go over my ideas before you make a final decision. I'll call you tomorrow at 11:50 a.m. to set up our meeting. Have a good day.

Wendy Winner, Sales Pro
XYZ International
555-555-2032
winnerw@.com

Your Turn

Now it's your turn. Write an e-mail using all the right and wrong techniques you have seen in Sam and Wendy's examples.

E-MAIL CONTENT

Your second and third e-mails should have a structure similar to that of the voice mails you left for Mr. Target, or you can alternate between voice mail and e-mail if you have both means of contact. Again, if you receive no calls or responses to your first two e-mails, send the goodbye e-mail as your third. File them in your follow-up file for the next quarter and add them to your e-newsletter (or hard-copy newsletter) distribution list so that they begin receiving regular news and updates from your company, building value and credibility for you over time.

The truth is that this prospect may not be in sufficient pain or at a point where he needs what you are offering just now. You want to stay in touch with him frequently enough to remain at the top of his mind when his pain or need becomes extreme. Then he'll reach out to you.

You don't want to be annoying, so be prudent in your approach timing. For example, don't even consider approaching a certified public accountancy (CPA) or bookkeeping firm during tax season. Make sure you understand your target's calendar timing so that you're not trying to get through during a month when they have zero time to spare for you. You'd look clueless, and your professional reputation would suffer irreparable damage.

◆◆◆

One more call is often the difference between success and failure.

OPENING STATEMENT MASTERY WORKSHOP

Now it's time for you to write one or more opening statements for selling situations you will encounter, such as the following:

- Speaking directly with your target on your first attempt.
- The decision maker interrupts to say she's late for a meeting or on her way to the airport.
- The insistent gatekeeper who must know "What is this in reference to?"
- Voice mail rather than live contact.
- Transfer to another person or an alternative decision maker.

Write your script so that when you deliver it, it flows naturally. You need to get to your benefits within the first 10 seconds and then relate your contact and credibility information without rushing.

Here's a quick list of where we are so far. Tell your prospects the following:

- Your name
- Your company
- Your phone number
- The benefit statement that gets their attention, focusing on the pain you identified in your research
- Company news or activities you read about recently, particularly as they pertain to your product or service
- What you are selling—in simple English
- What you want to do next (set appointment, direct to website, talk by telephone)
- Invitation to contact you if they would like
- Your name and phone number again
- Conclusion: something like good-bye, have a great day, enjoy the weekend, enjoy the nice weather

Sales Pro Tips

Here are some more tips for you:

- You are not trying to get the decision maker to write you a check with your opening statements; your prime objective is to grab his attention and open the door for an appointment, which then leads to more in-depth discussions.
- Refer to your notes from the behavior and learning models in Chapter 1 to create a custom statement that will put your targeted prospect in the center of the bull's-eye.
- Make every second of the call count.
- Every word and pause must have impact. Don't waste anything.
- If your statement has any tongue-twister phrases or words that you stumble over, reword it so that you can speak easily, without anxiety.

- If it's worth it to your employer for you to be calling, it is worthwhile for you to put the effort into writing and delivering the entire opening statement.
- You have no reason to be deceptive or sly. Misleading your target at this point will backfire every time. There is never a reason to trick a target into wanting to work with you.
- Keep your language simple without sounding condescending or foolish.
- Quell your own inner FUD. Your prospect *needs* you. You have a great product and a legitimate reason for calling, so tell her that with confidence.

PUTTING IT ALL TOGETHER

On the next several pages you will find script builder worksheets for voice mail messages, live phone calls, and e-mail messages. There are additional worksheets in Appendix H for you to photocopy or download and print.

Gatekeeper Script: Information Call

Hello, this is _____ from [your company].

    [Gatekeeper's name], could you please tell me who is the person who makes decisions about _____?

    Would you mind spelling that for me, please?

    What is [prospect name's] title? _____

    What is the best time to reach him? _____

    Could you give me her e-mail address? _____

    Does he have a direct phone number or an extension? _____

    I have her office address as _____.

    Is that correct? Is there a mail stop or floor number I should add?

_____

_____

Gatekeeper Script Variation: Voice Mail Option

Hello, [gatekeeper's name if you know it]. This is _____
from [your company].

    Is _____ *in?*

    Gatekeeper: *No. May I put you through to his voice mail?*

    Instead of answering the gatekeeper's question, ask your own questions to get some additional information. Revert to the first gatekeeper script to get correct spelling of names, full titles, e-mail addresses, best times to catch the decision maker, and whether this is the person you should be calling or if there is someone else who might be better qualified and authorized to speak with you. At this point, don't leave a voice mail. You're not ready, and your approach letter hasn't been sent.

Decision Maker Call Script: First Call

Timing: two or three days after your approach letter was mailed.

    Hi, [gatekeeper's name]. This is _____ *from [your company]. Is* _____ *in? Could I speak with her for just a minute?*

    (If gatekeeper asks, say: "Yes, she is expecting my call.")

    Decision maker picks up the line.

    Mr. D-M, I'm [your name] from [your company]. I'm calling to introduce myself and learn more about your [point of pain] and talk about how we might work together, increase your efficiency, and decrease your costs. [pause briefly]

    Is now a good time for a quick five-minute conversation? Great.

    (If it is not a good time, set a time for a return call. Follow up with an e-mail to confirm the call.)

    Can you tell me a little about your business and your goals?

_____

_____

    Then be quiet, listen, and take notes, clarifying any unclear points quickly. Do not launch into a sales pitch now, as it's not appropriate and you're not ready.

I'd like to send you some information about our solutions for your [point of pain and challenges], then touch base in a couple days to see when we might get together. [pause for two beats] Are you currently in the market for [products/services/solutions] like ours? _____

_____

I have your address as [street, city, state, zip] and your name as _____ *[spell it, even easy ones], and your title as* _____. *Is that correct?*

Thank you for taking time out of your busy day to speak with me. I'll get that information in the mail to you today.

Have a great day! Good-bye.

Here are the next steps:

- Don't spend more than three or four minutes on the phone so that you don't completely derail the person's day.
- Get your promised information assembled and into the mail (with a cover letter).
- Update your approach and their contact information in your CRM system.
- Send a LinkedIn invitation to the decision maker right now.

Decision Maker Call Script: Follow-Up to Packet Call

Timing: two or three days after mailing the packet of information you promised.

Hi, [gatekeeper's name]. This is _____ *from [your company]. Is* _____ *in? Could I please speak with him for just a minute?*

(If gatekeeper asks, say: "Yes, he is expecting my call.")

Mr. D-M, this is [your name] from [your company]. Have you received our information packet on [solution] to [their point of pain]? [pause] Have you looked at it?

Yes, the person has looked over the packet. Give him a second or so to get it and add any comments or observations he may have rather than jumping immediately to the next step. Listening throughout these steps is invaluable. Make notes about their comments.

What questions can I answer for you?

Answer his questions, or if you don't know, say so and promise to get back to him within a day with the answer. Then move to one of the alternative conclusions below.

Conclusion 1

Well, when could we get together briefly so I can show you more about how [our product/service/solution] can [cure your pain or solve your issues]?

Would Tuesday or Wednesday be better? _____

*Would morning or afternoon work better?*_____

How about [give them two times to choose from]:

9:30 *a.m. or* 11:00 *a.m.* _____ ?

2:00 *p.m. or* 3:30 *p.m.* _____ ?

Thank you so much, Mr. Decision Maker. I really appreciate your time today, and I'm looking forward to seeing you [repeat the time, day, and date]. *Have a great day.*

Here are the next steps:

- Update your CRM information.
- Send Ms. Decision Maker an e-mail thank-you note confirming your meeting.
- Move on to the next call.

Conclusion 2

They didn't look at the packet or haven't received it yet.

If they didn't have a chance to look at the packet, try the following:

While we're on the phone, let's open the packet and go through it quickly together so I can answer your questions.

Walk her through the packet briefly. Answer her questions or if you don't know, say so and promise to get back to her within a day with the answer. Then move on to set the appointment.

Well, when could we get together briefly so I can show you more about how [our product/service/solution] can [cure your pain or solve your issues]?

Would Tuesday or Wednesday be better? _____

Would morning or afternoon work better? _____

How about [give them two times to choose from]:

9:30 a.m. or 11:00 a.m. _____?

2:00 p.m. or 3:30 p.m. _____?

Thank you so much, Ms. Decision Maker. I really appreciate your time today, and I'm looking forward to seeing you [repeat the time, day and date]. *Have a great day.*

Here are the next steps:

- Update your CRM information.
- Send Mr. Decision-Maker an e-mail thank you note confirming your meeting.
- Move on to the next call.

If they didn't get the packet, try the following:

I'm so sorry; let me send another to you. (Or courier it to them, if feasible.)

[Confirm their address one more time] _____

_____

I'll call you back when you have received the packet. Again, my apologies. Have a great day.

◆◆◆

Sales execution is everything.

OBJECTION HANDLING

Accept the reality of objections at every step of the sales cycle; they go with the territory. In fact, objections are a good thing because they show that the decision maker is involved and is working through a thought process with you.

Some objections will be creative, but most objections you'll encounter will be repeats. Your secret weapon is having an arsenal of ready responses so that you can deflect the objections and continue to move the process forward.

You will encounter eight key objections during the appointment approach process as well as throughout the entire sales cycle. It is better to field them early in the process so that you can reduce them to rubble right away:

1. The prospect doesn't perceive the *value* in your product or service.
2. There is no *urgency* on the part of the prospect for buying your proposal.
3. The prospect sees your offer as inferior to your *competitor's offer*.
4. *Power struggles* internally between individuals or departments are sabotaging the sale.
5. *No money* or budget is available for purchasing.
6. The decision maker has *personality conflicts or adverse experiences* with the internal recommender or the sales professional.
7. A *preexisting relationship with an outside third party* is creating roadblocks to working with you.
8. The company or decision maker suffers from an *inability to make decisions*; it's safer to do nothing than to be decisive.

No doubt the last one will be the most troublesome and difficult to overcome. This is where persistence comes into play. You keep approaching the decision maker over time and see what other influencers and/or decision makers higher up the ladder you can involve to move the decision forward. Don't give up.

Here are a few pointers to help with understanding and handling objections in the SMART Prospecting process:

- Welcome any objections you receive from your prospects. They're confirming that they have a need or are experiencing a pain that your product or service may solve. It is your response—your words and attitude—that now determines where this sales cycle will end.

- Understand what they're saying with their objection even if it's the 9,500th time you have heard the same thing from the same prospect. These are the easy ones to handle: it's the oddball objections that will trip you up if you don't have a good response. Once you fully understand the objection, you can map out the next steps for this particular sales prospect; this is much like solving a puzzle. Now you have another clue to work with.
- Confirm the objection by repeating it back to the prospect. Ask whatever questions you need to clarify the objection before moving forward. Acknowledge what the prospect is saying without judging. No sighing, no eye rolling (even on the phone), no change in tone that signifies your exasperation. Your patience and professional demeanor are your most effective tools.
- Be direct in responding to the objection. Leave sarcasm or unnecessarily flip and humorous responses behind and face the objection head on. If you are defensive or evasive or avoid the objection and manipulate the prospect, it will result in a lost opportunity.
- Defuse the objection by using your never-fail responses to get to the heart of the issue and continue your forward progress.

Once you understand the real objection you're facing, you will be able to map out the next steps. Depending on the objections conversation, you may be moving to the next part of the sales cycle. Or you may realize that the prospect's pain isn't sufficient to require your attention at the moment or that the prospect is one of the 80 percent who do not belong in your sales funnel. In that case, spend your time on more worthwhile targets.

OBJECTION MASTERY

Here's how you can handle the most common objections:

Prospect: Not at this time, not really in the market, too busy right now, still gathering information, stall or objection, other nonaffirmative responses.

Sales Pro: Your task here is to understand the verbalized objection (usually money or time), check for red flags, and make sure the prospect wants to meet (despite the objection) and sincerely wants to proceed with you.

Prospect: The timing isn't right.

Sales Pro: "I certainly understand that your budget/time may be tight at the moment, but I also know that you really would like to [try this product, take advantage of this offer, use our service]. Is that right?"

Listen to their comments to decide if they are stalling or if they sincerely have an issue with or objection to meeting in the near future.

Sales Pro: "Well, I don't want to miss getting this [information/product/one-time chance] in front of you. Is there a time—even outside of normal business hours—that we might meet, perhaps for a coffee break, in the evening, or . . . ?"

What should you say if the prospect says he may buy from a competitor?

The following series of questions will help you weed out and disqualify those who are wasting your time and are not likely to buy from you.

If someone says that she usually buys from a competitor of yours but would like to see your information, say the following:

Sales Pro: "I'd be happy to send our information, but just out of curiosity, why might you think about working with or trying another vendor?"

Acknowledge the answer neutrally regardless of what it is and then say:

Sales Pro: Okay. If you like what you see or try, then what happens?

Gauge the response once again but don't react negatively to whatever she says.

Next you ask:

Sales Pro: How many other companies have you considered for this [service/product] in the last six months?

Then ask one final question:

Sales Pro: Which of these did you do business with?

Then it's your decision, based on your instincts and the answers gathered here, whether to send information about your product or service to the prospect.

Multiple Objections in Succession

If you're getting yet another objection—must talk to someone (you should be meeting with the decision maker since that was part of your qualifying process, right?), major announcement coming, and so on—it should be a red flag that this isn't going anywhere anytime soon. Cut your losses, get agreement for future follow-up, and move on.

Sales Pro: Well, what I will do then is to keep your information close by and give you a call in, say, two or three months. Will that work for you?
Prospect: Yes, that would be fine.
Sales Pro: Thank you so much, Ms. Decision Maker. I really appreciate your time today. I'll speak with you again soon. Have a great day.

Hang up, update your CRM information, and move confidently on to the next call.

◆◆◆

Manage your prospects and clients up or out. Don't waste
time on lost causes.

CUTTING YOUR LOSSES

After a couple of your dynamite voice mails have been ignored, try contacting the all-powerful gatekeeper or administrative assistant again (you have a record of her or his name, right?) and ask for help in seeing if there is a time or day when you might have success talking with Ms. Target live. Something like this usually works:

"Hi, Pat. It's Wendy Winner from Widget World. I'm hoping you can help me: I've been trying to get Mr. Target on the phone, and I keep missing him. Any ideas about when is the best time and day to reach him?" [Pause for a second as if this just occurred to you.] *"Or is there another number I could try, like his cell phone, maybe, or his e-mail?"*

Remember to thank Pat genuinely for whatever information you receive even if it's completely unhelpful. You want the gatekeeper always thinking nice things about you. Don't burn that bridge.

◆◆◆

The more human and relatable you are with people, the harder it is
for them to say no to you.

Despite your best efforts and your following this plan to the letter, Mr. Target may not grasp the business-booming implications of your messages and may never call you back. In that event, you need to cut your losses after the third call. You have much better prospects to give your return on investment increaser to, and if Mr. Target isn't interested, there are plenty who are in pain and need you. You now leave one last voice mail message that says good-bye nicely but in no uncertain terms.

Good-Bye, So Long Example: Voice Mail 3

Sales Pro: "Hello, Mr. Target. It's Wendy Winner from WidgetWorld, 555 [pause] 522 [pause] 5555. I have left you several messages with no response, and at this point I will conclude that you have no current need or interest in increasing your ROI [or profit, or efficiencies] at this time. [pause for comprehension] If I have misunderstood, please call me at your earliest convenience so I can give you more details. Again, this is Wendy Winner, and my direct number is 555 [pause] 522 [pause] 5555."

E-mail Follow-Up 3

Mr. Target,

I just left you a voice mail and thought I would follow up with a quick e-mail to make one last contact with you. (Obviously, do not use this sentence if you did not leave a voice mail.)

I have left you several messages with no response, and at this point I will conclude that you have no current need or interest in increasing your ROI [or profit or efficiencies] at this time.

I will place you on our newsletter mailing list and contact you again in two or three months to see if you are ready at that time to meet.

If I have misunderstood, please call me or send me an e-mail at your earliest convenience so I can give you more details.

Wendy Winner, Account Executive
Widget World Enterprises, Inc.
Direct line: 555-522-5555
E-mail: wendy.winner@.com

Bottom line: Once you start using the SMART Prospecting methodology, it's critical that you remain consistent. You're building trust and reliability by calling at the precise time you stated in your letter. Connect with them on LinkedIn and Twitter and always lead with value or a news article that you saw in your research. By leveraging all the social media tools available today and being traditional by sending a letter, you will be successful.

◆ ◆ ◆

Get rid of your worst client or your least promising prospect today.

CHAPTER 8

♦♦♦

OBJECTIVES ARE CLOSER
THAN THEY APPEAR

[A]s you've noticed, people don't want to be sold.
What people do want is news and information about
the things they care about.[1]

LARRY WEBER

The golden day has finally come: you're ready to meet with your prospect. If you have followed the steps outlined in this book and prepared yourself, you have already won the business and are ready for the call.

I believe in overpreparing for every call, and I encourage you to do that too. When I was providing service to attorneys to New Hampshire, I talked with a junior associate at the firm before I had met all the partners. I knew the junior associate was not the ultimate decision maker, but we started a great relationship and I was managing the sales process. It was a cold day in January when I arrived at the firm and was met by the junior associate with whom I thought I was meeting one on one. We exchanged pleasantries, and then he said, "They're ready for us, Mike." I said, "Who is ready for us?" He replied that I was meeting with all five of the managing partners. I said "Great!" and though I was a little nervous, I walked in the room and completely changed my agenda. Luckily, I prepare for every call as if I were meeting with the president of any large company. I was prepared and answered all their questions. I asked, "So do you want to dominate the Internet or rent it?" The managing partners immediately responded with "Dominate!" I replied, "It will be $XXX, $XX per month," followed by silence. The managing partners said okay, and I closed the sale.

This story is important because if I had not been professional, prepared, and prompt, I guarantee they would have not signed that day. Be overprepared on every call. Do your homework.

By the way, it was the largest sale ever recorded in New Hampshire and still is to this day.

SALES PROFESSIONALS' BIGGEST MISTAKES

As was reported in the *Harvard Business Review*,[2] Tom Atkinson and Ron Koprowski surveyed 138 customers responsible for making business-to-business purchases for large North American companies in a variety of industries. Topping the list of mistakes were sales professionals' failure to follow the customer's buying processes and poor listening skills.

Resolve now to rectify any issues that you see in yourself. Your prospect may never tell you or anyone from your company why she didn't buy from you or didn't continue a business relationship with you.

Using LinkedIn Effectively

Here's how to make the best use of LinkedIn:

- Join LinkedIn and provide the overview information.
- Complete the employment and education history.
- Add a profile summary.
- Select an industry and add your specialties.
- Add your website or websites.
- Create a public profile URL.

- Confirm all e-mail addresses.
- Set your contact settings.
- Make introductions to connect via LinkedIn.
- Collect at least three recommendations from your "network."
- Give and you shall receive.

TEN TIPS ON BUILDING A STRONG PROFILE

Here are 10 ways to build a strong profile:

1. Don't cut and paste your résumé.
2. Borrow from the best marketers.
3. Write a personal tagline.
4. Put your elevator pitch to work.
5. Point out your skills.
6. Explain your experience.
7. Distinguish yourself from the crowd.
8. Ask and answer questions.
9. Add content that will help with search engine optimization (SEO).
10. Build your connections.

Ask questions of contacts you discover that help you get your work done. Don't ask about the people they know but about the knowledge they have. Any question that allows subject matter experts to share their knowledge will produce more answers and will be welcomed by other users. Questions that ask for introductions, partners, clients, and contacts produce substantially fewer answers. Users may flag these types of questions as inappropriate. When a question is flagged by several users, it is automatically removed and reviewed. Users who have many flagged questions may be blocked from asking more questions.

If you are asking a question to recruit or advertise or are announcing your own job search, you must indicate that while creating the question with the checkboxes provided.

Here are some things LinkedIn recommends to protect your privacy:

1. Connect only to people you know and trust well enough to recommend them to others. This gives you much more control over who can see your profile and who can contact you. It also makes it far more likely that introduction requests that are forwarded to you will be in line with your interests. Because your direct connections are able to see your most up-to-date primary e-mail address, connecting only to people you trust will help you keep your contact information safe.

2. Don't post your e-mail address, phone number, or other addresses on your LinkedIn profile; if you do, you'll have much less control over how your contact information can be used.

3. Familiarize yourself with your current personal privacy and contact settings on LinkedIn so that you know what they are and what options you have. To view these settings, visit Account and Settings at the top of your home page.

4. Select a password for LinkedIn that can't easily be guessed. Create one that includes 10 or more characters and includes both letters and numbers.

5. Never give your LinkedIn password to others.

6. If you use a public or shared computer to log on to LinkedIn, make sure to log out completely when you've finished.

7. Report privacy problems that you see or experience on LinkedIn to the customer service help center.

Bottom line: Join LinkedIn today and start connecting.

CHAPTER 9

◆◆◆

SOUP TO NUTS

What follows is an actual sales process manual that we prepared for one of our recent clients. The names and other nonessential details have been changed to protect the company's competitive advantage.

THE SELLING GROUP SALES PROCESS

The Selling Group sales process is based on the Sales Sense System and will always be a work in progress and require ongoing "tweaking" to consistently improve the process.

Objective: To increase sales for Selling Team by systematically going after the market and leveraging a proven sales process.

Selling Team, an Innovative Billing and IT Solutions Company.

Why Selling Team? Win with competitive advantages in the marketplace. Selling Team is a different type of IT solutions and billing company. We focus on bringing you software and IT solutions that build relationships and deliver a competitive advantage through:

- Costs Leadership, where Selling Team helps you achieve lower costs of doing business
- Rapid response to changing market and customer conditions
- Differentiation in the marketplace affords you a unique value proposition (UVP)

Our Vision: To be the preeminent leader in consulting and subscription billing solutions by using our knowledge to uncover insights that create unprecedented value for our clients.

Our Mission: To leverage our efficiencies and transformational capabilities to create a sustainable competitive advantage for our clients and set the standard for operational excellence.

The secret to Selling Team's success is our *people*, our *products*, and our *philosophy*.

Rules of engagement: be organized, have multiple screens open, and be in a quiet environment.

YOUR COMPUTER VIEW

Google (For companies' websites), CRM (Zoho), LinkedIn, News source: Indeed, Yahoo–Finance, CIO, Information Week, Lead 411, and Sales Genie. Tip: Open a Twitter account and follow your news/information sources and eliminate all the other screens.

Potential lead sources: Indeed, Deloitte, LinkedIn job boards, and LinkedIn Groups.

Focus should be just like you're driving a sports car: brake, clutch, gas, shift, gas, clutch, shift, and gas.

Computer screen should have the following up and ready:

Brake: CRM—The "brake" is your slowdown. It's critical to stop and capture all of your information. "Stop and smell the roses." Capture the mood of the caller and any sales intelligence from the call. Best time to call back, any pressing news or information on their website. Cut and paste the news with the link that you found on their site or on Google to your notes section in your CRM. This way when a person picks up the phone (a miracle) you will be ready to switch gears and speak to current events and news that pertains to their business.

Clutch: Your screen—Have the following up at all times: LinkedIn, Twitter, Google, and their website. LinkedIn is a valuable tool to see if you're already connected to the prospect or are one away from the prospect and can name-drop if the prospect picks up. Look at the groups that the prospect is engaged in, and join the groups that make sense to join. Remember—people buy from people they can relate to, and the faster you find a common thread, the faster the prospect will become a client.

Check out all of their links on their profile, click on their website and view current news or events. Check out their Twitter and see what they have "tweeted" about and follow them. In an ideal situation they will follow you back and you will have a direct contact with them and able to communicate using Twitter as the medium. Once you have that direct connection it gets no better than that; it's fast and personal.

Gas: Your tone. Listen to the engine (prospect). It's important to pace and "mirror" your client's speed of talk and keep up with them or slow down. You never want to imitate an accent or speech; you just want to be speaking at the same pace. Do not pass the "pace car."

SALES PRO TIPS:

1. Be brief ➝ be excited ➝ be happy!!!!! ☺ Listen to yourself with your pace and tone. (option: mirror in front of you to watch facial expressions.)
2. Place a mirror in front of you and have your water near you as you call. (Do not drink when talking.) Stretch before you sit down and do some light jumping jacks to get the blood going. All of these small exercises make a difference in how you present yourself over the phone.

3. Sit straight in your chair and focus on what you are doing. You are meeting people for the first time through the phone, no different than in person; the first impressions are everything! Walk around when making calls and you will come across more excited. Close the door of your office to maintain complete silence around you. Add some light music in the background if you wish. No dogs, street noise, or doorbells, and please, no babies in the background.

4. If you are taking notes as you talk to people, make sure you have a quiet keyboard. Tone is everything on the phone.

5. Record your calls on your phone or a recording device and listen back to hear yourself speak.

SALES PROCESS STEPS

Step #1: Target market. It's critical to have a clear target for all of your campaigns; the more precise you become, the greater the results! For your first campaign the focus was: ABC plus in revenue and located in the XYZ area. As the campaign matures or a vertical is identified, I would recommend a vertical market penetration strategy that would focus on the identified vertical with a wider net. Suggested criteria for campaigns: sales, geography, employee, industry, title. Salesgenie is the identified database that data will be "pulled" in a CSV [comma-separated values] format.

Step #2: Enter data in Zoho and set up a separate campaign with a clear and identifiable title, i.e., Date and Target. Double check the data after the upload is complete and "clean." It's important to keep a tidy database for reporting and tracking purposes.

Step #3: Call the general phone number of each company and clarify the decision maker. If gatekeeper answers the phone with their first name, repeat their name back to them to create a common bond.

"Hi [gatekeeper name], this is [sales professional name]. If you could be so kind to direct me to the appropriate person who handles . . . (pause)"

Or

"Hello, this is [sales professional name] from Selling Team, If you could be so kind as to direct me to the person that would make decisions (in charge of) with regard to IT or billing?" (Record in Zoho)

Sales Pro: "Hi, _____. How's your day? (Pause) I was curious to whom I could speak with regard to IT or billing."

"Who makes decisions with _____? Can I have an e-mail address?" (Always try to get something from the call. Do not call just to call. Obtain business intelligence on each and every call.)

Obtain decision maker and e-mail: (Record in Zoho)

If decision maker picks up, have a small conversation and tell them you will be sending out a letter that outlines your services; and if they are open, keep chatting and see if they are in the market for Selling Team's product offering. . . . Thank you very much!

After decision maker is identified based on the data from Salesgenie, Google their name and see what comes up. Look for a Twitter account and follow them or the company to keep up-to-date with your prospect. Register their name in Google Alerts along with their name and add in the search box: "name of prospect" and the word "says." This will keep you informed on all of the quotes he/she has mentioned out on the Internet and keep you informed. It's powerful to mention you saw an article and you enjoyed what they said.

Step #4: Send out letter to clarified decision maker. You can use the "Circle of Leverage." If the company appears to have multiple layers, it may be necessary to send out three letters to the company, addressing it to three identified people in the company. This will "leverage" the relationship in your targeted prospect account. The reason that this is powerful is that no one wants to be caught "sleeping at the wheel," i.e., not doing their job. Always copy the "top dog" at the organization in your letters.

SALES PRO TIPS:

1. Always copy the top dog. CC: all people that you sent the letter to.
2. Be specific with the date and time you will be calling.

3. Hand address each envelope. (Use Avery 5160 [labels] for mass mailing.)
4. Include a business card.
5. Sign each letter.
6. First-class stamp only, not metered.
7. If a priority, use FedEx or DHL.
8. Set specific times in your calendar that you mentioned in the letter (10 to 15 minutes apart).
9. Follow the process and be detailed with your notes.

SALES SENSE LETTER FRAMEWORK

Below is a brief outline of a Sales Sense letter followed by a sample letter that employs this structure.

Grabber
Decision maker
Research your account.
Pain: What is their pain or what would make them happy?
Frustrated with?
Curiosity
What if _____ what would this mean to your business _____ 10–30 percent increase in revenue or reduction in time or cost?
Results: Be specific with your results.
Articulate
What have other clients achieved by your services?
Result of using our services: Our clients have saved over (10–20% in time using our system, which has resulted in less turnover and _____ to the bottom line.)
Why would they buy?
Be very specific about the results.
Unique
UVP

Unique value proposition: I help (target) solve (key need/want) by
(what you do).

Why buy you?

Why do people buy from you?

Think!

If you went out of business today, what would people miss?

Testimonial in a similar industry; try to make the testimonial
industry-specific.

Title: Try to have the title match the title of the decision maker on
this letter.

Ideal

Where was the client before your services, and where are they now
after your services?

Next Steps

Control/Control the next steps in your sales process.

Be specific

Tell them exactly when you will be calling: I will call you at
HH:MM M/D/Y.

Closing

Name, e-mail, and phone number for them to reach you.

SAMPLE LETTER TO PROSPECT

Frustrated with your current IT projects? Do you feel that with the right team
the project could have been completed by now and delivered the results you
expected?

Companies that leverage superior IT capabilities gain a competitive
advantage in the marketplace. Does your IT department deliver a competitive advantage? An effective IT department will respond promptly to
changing market conditions, augment product differentiation, and provide
internal cost leadership to maximize your profits. Does this describe your IT
department?

Selling Team has achieved the following results in connection with our
most recent projects:

- Ingenuity in execution: Over $1,000,000 saved on Billing Systems implementation plan
- Operational excellence: Revenue assurance policies compressing financial close by 50%.
- Maximum profitability: Turn up services sooner with a 25% reduced service delivery cycle time.

What makes Selling Team unique from all others?

Ingenuity in execution: We deliver imaginative solutions for successful and cost-effective results.

Unparalleled integration: Our services result in seamless operation of your IT systems.

Operational excellence: The integration we achieve provides for operation with the highest efficiency.

Maximum profitability: Delivered to you! Profitability and sustainable competitive advantages!

Does your IT Partner deliver these results?

How our clients praise Selling Team . . .

"I thought our billing system was archaic and needed to be replaced. Jacob and his team used their ingenuity and innovations to not only salvage our legacy billing system, but transitioned it into a competitive advantage for us, while saving us hundreds of thousands of dollars." CEO, I will call you on July 17, 2012, at 4:15 p.m. to introduce myself and discover more about your business and how we can work together to help you achieve success.

Respectfully,

Step #5: Engagement is critical in the sales process. You will have only a few seconds to make a first impression with the prospect, and you need to be prompt, professional, and prepared.

Sales Pro Tips:

1. *Prompt*—Call at exactly the time you stated in the letter.
2. *Professional*—Be friendly and welcoming to all gatekeepers.

3. *Be to the point*—Avoid long-winded and pointless responses.
4. *Practice your message* before you make your first call.
5. *Prepared*—Be ready for the prospect to pick up the phone.

Purpose—Purpose of your call; be specific when calling and say it up front! "The purpose of my call is to . . . set an appointment, send you information, invite you to a webinar, or invite you to a seminar."

Process—Know your process; be able to articulate the process to your prospect. "I would suggest the following process to understand each other's companies and see if there is a strategic fit for us to work together. . . . Let's meet casually and just have an open conversation and discover more about each other. Does this sound fair?"

Payoff—Know the payoff for your prospect. WIIFM—What's in it for me? "By us meeting casually first we will be able to vet out any issues/challenges and set up next steps without all decision makers being present, saving us both time and energy, and at this point I'm not sure I can even help you. Sound fair?"

Gatekeeper picks up—"This is [sales professional] from Selling Team. Is First Name in? (Pause)

GK: "What's this regarding?"

You: "We have exchanged correspondence; please tell him/her that this is [sales professional] on the line from Selling Team calling at the precise time that I had mentioned to him/her."

GK: "Are they expecting your call?"

You: "Yes, he/she is expecting my call." (Pause)

OPTION #1:

Prospect accepts your call: "This is [Prospect Name]."

Sales Pro: "Hi, [Prospect Name]. Thanks for taking my call. I know your time is valuable, and the purpose of my call is to discover more about you and your IT or billing challenges (identified pain). I noticed in (source-article) that . . . [or] that your CEO stated in your annual report. . . . Did you see the article or statement?" (Pause)

Prospect: "No."

You: "That's okay; it's hard to keep up with all the communications at your company. I will send you the article via e-mail so you can have it as a reference. What I'd love to do is just meet briefly face-to-face over coffee or at your office and learn more about you and address any challenges you might be facing in today's competitive environment.

"How's your calendar next Tuesday or Thursday? Morning or afternoon? 10 or 11? 1 or 3?" (long pause)

Prospect: "What's this about?"

Sales Pro: "As stated in my letter: As a company, we offer you services that are of the highest standard at extremely competitive rates. Selling Team can assist in integrating data from different platforms and establishing efficient data warehousing, developing an IT department that achieves much more than merely keeping the network operating. Our cutting edge client relationship and billing software provide a cost-effective and problem-free solution for serving your clients throughout the customer life cycle. We also provide first-rate consulting and outsourcing services that will stay within your budget

"I'm not asking you to change from your current provider. What I am asking for is an opportunity to discover more about you and your business, because as of right now, I'm not sure I can help you. It's always good to have a plan B in case your current relationship goes awry, wouldn't you agree?

"How's your calendar next Tuesday or Thursday? Morning or Afternoon? 10:00 or 11:00? 1:00 or 3:00?" (long pause—silence)

Prospect: "Tuesday at 10:00."

Sales Pro: "Great! I am excited to help you with your current IT challenges; I will be sending you a brief e-mail confirming our appointment with some additional information. What is your e-mail? I have your address as. . . . Correct? Any special instructions to gain access to your building?

"Do you have any questions for me? Thank you again for taking the time out of your busy day to speak with me, I look forward to meeting with you at: [repeat time back]."

Immediately send e-mail to prospect as stated and put all information in Zoho.

Record in your calendar and send your prospect an invite so you are on their calendar as well.

OPTION #2:

Sales Pro: "Hello, [prospect name]. This is [sales professional] from Selling Team. How are you today? I'll be brief. And this is not a sales call.

"The purpose of my call is to introduce myself and learn more about your company's IT and billing challenges (pain) and set a time to meet face-to-face and discuss how we can work together to increase efficiency and profits. I know you get a lot of these calls, don't you? (Pause) Maybe even laugh with them. . . . Let me share with you how we are you unique. . .

"Selling Team offers services of the highest standard at extremely competitive rates. We specialize in integrating data from different platforms, data migration, data warehousing, and general IT department development. Our featured solution is cutting-edge client relationship management and billing software that provide an extremely cost-effective and problem-free solution for serving your clients throughout the entire customer life cycle. We understand that you may already have a relationship with a service provider, and we are not asking you to make a change at this time, but it's always good to have a backup plan. What I am asking for is 15 to 30 minutes of your time to discover more about you and your business. I happen to be in your area next Tuesday or Thursday of next week.

"Which day is better for you?" (Long pause—silence)

OPTION #3:

Use Mr. and Mrs. Name . . .

Sales Pro: "This is [sales professional] with Selling Team, I promise to be brief. We are an innovative billing and IT solutions company. The purpose of my call is to connect at the time I promised you in my letter and introduce myself and learn more about your current business challenges and discuss leveraging your IT to establish sustainable competitor advantages (increase profit).

"This is not a sales call. We have had a tremendous amount of success in IT. I'm not sure if we can even be of help to you yet." [Name-drop any current clients]

"Let me ask you a few brief questions. . . .

"Are you experiencing any of the following?

[or] "On a scale of 1–10, 10 being an urgent need to get done today and 1 being it can wait until next 12 months:

- Is your billing solution a "game changer"? We can cut your cost by 50%.
- Do you find that year after year your costs are going up per invoice?
- How would you describe your data analytics? Lack of effectively managing data into a viewable and usable format . . .
- What do you do now to effectively leverage your data?
- What's your typical cycle time from order to revenue recognition?
- Can you tell me service delivery cycle time?
- Do you find that you are experiencing high customer churn?
- Cost per bill?
- Tell me more about your ERP [enterprise resource planning] supply chain?

"I'm not asking you to change from your current provider. What I am asking is an opportunity to discover more about you and your business and share what some of your competitors are doing to create a competitive advantage with information technology. It's always good to have a plan B in case your current relationship goes awry. Wouldn't you agree?

"I'm open next Tuesday and Thursday. How's your calendar? Morning or afternoon? 10:00 or 11:00? 1:00 or 3:00?" (long pause)
Prospect: "Tuesday at 10:00."

Sales Pro: "Great! I am excited to discuss your current IT challenges; I will be sending you a brief e-mail confirming our appointment with some additional information. What is your e-mail?

"Do you have any questions for me? Thank you again for taking the time out of your busy day to speak with me. I look forward to meeting with you at: [repeat time back]."

THE CLOSE: IF PROSPECT ASKS YOU ANY QUESTIONS

Sales Pro: "Great question! You know [prospect name], we find the best way to address all of your questions is a face-to-face meeting. I will make you three promises, [prospect name]:

1. I will keep to the time that we agree upon, usually 30 minutes.
2. This is not a sales call; the purpose of our first call is information ONLY! And finally . . .
3. At this point, I do not know if I can help you or not. I do not know enough about your business to make a decision, and you do not know enough about our solutions to make a decision. At the end of our call, we will agree together and make an informed decision about what the next step is to continue our relationship or part as friends. . . . How is your calendar next Tuesday or Thursday, morning or afternoon, 10:00 a.m. or 11:00 a.m., 1:00 p.m., or 2:00 p.m.?" (long pause)

Options:

Gatekeeper: "What's this regarding?"

"We have exchanged correspondence, and he/she is expecting my call at [Mention the specific time in your letter].

"Selling Team is an innovative billing and IT company. We specialize in integrating data across various platforms, establishing data warehousing, providing first-rate consulting services, and assisting with outsourcing.

"We feature Bill Force, a state-of-the-art customer service and billing solution."

[If you have relevant information, such as an article or news, please talk about the article.]

"I'm on your website, and I'm still trying to get my arms around your business and current challenges. When it comes to IT and data integration, what would make your job easier?"

MORE INFORMATION REQUEST:

First clarify what type of information:

Sales Pro: "I would love to send you some additional information. What specifically are you looking for?" or "What are your current challenges?"

E-mail to send:

Subject line: As promised from (Sales Pro) or per your request.

Dear _____:

I enjoyed our conversation today, and I look forward to meeting you in person soon. Please review our case study section on our site; I think you will find the information helpful to you and your organization.

I read this article the other day from *Harvard Business Review*, and I wanted to share it with you.

I'm available for any additional questions; I will follow up next Tuesday.

Enjoy the rest of your day.

Respectfully,

APPOINTMENT INVITATION AND SOCIAL MEDIA INTEGRATION:

Step 1: Subject Line: As promised from [Sales Pro]

To _____:

Thank you again for your time today. I look forward to meeting with you on _____ at your office. Please have your questions ready, and feel free to invite any other people involved on your team to the meeting.

I look forward to learning more about you and your business.

Respectfully,

Step 2: Send a LinkedIn invite to the person you set an appointment with.

To _____:

Thank you again for your time today. Please accept my LinkedIn invitation to view my background.

Respectfully,

Step 3: Additional social media to follow: YouTube, Twitter, Google+, and Pinterest. The purpose of following your prospect is to find relevant information that will either identify their current pain or solve a problem and make their lives easier, making them happier! People buy from people, and the more you can find out about them, the better. If you like fishing and they like fishing, you will end up having a more relevant and meaningful business conversation. Sources for information to post on your personal social media:

http://mashable.com

http://alltop.com

http://www.hubspot.com

Option: Send out a confirmation letter or note card with the appointment reminder enclosed.

Step 4: "The voice mail and e-mail game": not available or goes to voice mail. Rules of engagement: The first wave of messaging goes out after three business days (longer if mailing a greater distance). All calls are followed up two business days after message is left. (On average it takes two business days to return a voice mail.) If no response after the messaging sequence, put them in your drip campaign or a call back in 90 days.

Sales Pro Tips:

1. Be consistent with your message.
2. Don't sound "canned."
3. Practice, practice, practice.
4. Leave yourself a voice mail and listen to how you sound.
5. Be excited with your message with a hint of mystery (curiosity).
6. Send out e-mail immediately after voice mail.
7. If you have a fax number, send them the same e-mail message via fax.
8. If you are connected via social media, send them a message (Twitter/ Direct Message).
9. Have e-mail messaging ready to go and integrated with Zoho.
10. Leave your phone number twice: once in the beginning and once near the end.

FIRST VOICE MAIL—VM #1

Hello, [prospect]. This is [sales pro] with Selling Team—the premier billing & IT solutions company. My direct number is 555–522–5555.

As promised, I am calling you as mentioned in the letter I sent you this week. The purpose of my call is to introduce myself to you and learn more about your billing and IT initiatives needs at _____. Please call me at your earliest convenience and I can give you more details about our unique solutions to help you achieve your strategic goals.

Again, this is _____, and my number is 555–552–5045.

(Option) State you will call them in the afternoon again.

IMMEDIATELY SEND E-MAIL #1:

Subject: Per my voice mail.

Hello «Salutation» «Last Name»:

I hope all is well. I am just checking with you to determine if you got the message I left you. I would love to connect with you and learn more about your challenges with your billing and IT infrastructure.

I am sure you are busy, so I am trying not to bother you with too much follow-up until the time is right for you.

All IT business services are not created equal. Here are some of our advantages compared to other "IT" companies:

- *Integrated billing*—Transparency, flexibility, and reliability across all sales to cash processes, reducing your cost by more than half.
- *Ingenuity*—Let us help you identify and overcome your challenges, transforming them into sustainable competitive advantages.
- *Profitability*—Selling Team is a proven provider of significant top and bottom line growth.

All I am asking for is a few minutes on the phone with you. If this sounds fair enough, please let me know the best time for us to talk.

How's this coming Thursday at 11:00 a.m.?

I enjoyed reading this article from *CIO*, and I wanted to share it with you: [link to article or attach the article.]

If there is a more appropriate person I should be contacting, I would appreciate it if you could forward me their contact information.

Respectfully,

SECOND VOICE MAIL—VM #2

Hello, [prospect]. This is [sales pro] with Selling Team, the premier billing and IT solutions company. My direct number is 555-522-5555.

I am just checking back with you to determine if you got the last voice mail I left you. If there is a more appropriate person I should be contacting, I would appreciate if you could forward me their contact information.

Option—I would like to ask you for a few minutes to discuss this over the phone with you. At this point, I certainly don't expect you to make any changes.

Option—I am planning on making a call to your senior management team and wanted your opinion before making the call.

Please call me at your earliest convenience and I can give you more details. Again, this is (sales pro), and my number is 555–522–5555.

IMMEDIATELY SEND E-MAIL #2

Subject: Follow up from [sales pro] or second request, a response is appreciated.

Hello «Salutation» «Last Name»:

I hope all is well. I'm just checking back with you to determine if you received the last couple of voice mails I left you. I am sure that things are quite hectic, so I am trying not to bother you with too much follow-up until the time is right for you.

I'd like to ask for a few minutes to discuss your current IT business challenges and the benefits of working with the Selling Group and myself. At this point, I certainly don't expect you to make any changes.

Please click here to view our case studies.

With Selling Team, we make it easy to work with us, and you will be pleased with the unique experience we deliver. How's next Thursday at 11:00 a.m. to connect via phone?

Respectfully,

THIRD VOICE MAIL—VM#3

Hello, [prospect]. This is [sales pro] with Selling Team—the premier billing and IT solutions company. My direct number is 555–522–5555.

I have left you several messages with no response, and at this point, I will conclude that there is no current need or interest with regard to increasing your efficiencies in your billing or IT department. If I have misunderstood this, please call me at your earliest convenience and I can give you more details. Again, this is _____ , and my number is 555-522-5555. Please visit us online at SellingGroup.com.

IMMEDIATELY SEND E-MAIL #3

Subject: Follow-up from [sales pro].

Hi «Salutation» «Last Name»:

I hope all is well. I have left you several e-mails and voice mails and have not received an answer. I would love to connect with you and learn more about your challenges with keeping your IT business as efficient as possible while reducing your overall cost.

All IT business services are not created equal. Here are some of our advantages compared to other "IT" companies:

- *Integrated billing*—transparency, flexibility, and reliability across all sales to cash processes, reducing your cost by more than half.
- *Ingenuity*—Let us help you identify and overcome your challenges, transforming them into competitive advantages.
- *Profitability*—Selling Team is a proven provider of significant top and bottom line growth.

As I have left you several messages with no response, at this point I will conclude that there is no current need or interest with regard to IT and business initiatives. If I have misunderstood this, please call me at your earliest convenience and I can give you more details.

I enjoyed reading this article and wanted to share it with you. . . .

I hope to work with you soon; enjoy the rest of your day.

Respectfully,

(LISTEN) It is very important in the beginning of the relationship that the customer/client/prospect feels they are being listened to and understood.

Ask only these questions: Can you tell me more? Why do you ask? How do you mean? You want to keep the prospect talking.

By using the above questions you are creating an open-ended conversation and they are talking. Try to have them talk 80% of the time. Avoid closed ended questions (yes or no answered questions).

Objection: "We Are Already in a Relationship."

Sales Pro: "I can certainly appreciate that you already have an existing relationship; the purpose of my call is to be your next choice if your current relationship was to go awry. I'm sure you would agree that having a solid plan B in place is critical in today's business environment. How's your calendar next week on Tuesday?"

Objection: "We Have No Issues."

Sales Pro: "That's fantastic! You're one of the lucky ones; most companies I speak with are in constant turmoil and are always looking for a better mousetrap and to increase profit. If you had a crystal ball, what would make your business life even easier?" (Pause)

Objection: Whatever Their Objection Is

Sales Pro: 1. Why do you ask?
2. Tell me more. . . .
3. Compared to what?
4. How do you mean?

The art of objection handling is: pause (clarify objection) and respond with a question back to them that makes sense.

OBJECTION RESPONSES

We're not a high-pressured sales organization. The first call is not a sales call. Let me send you some additional information on our solutions and go from there; does this sound fair?

We are not replacing your current staff; we're just helping them increase their productivity so they can work on other projects and be more efficient.

I know how you feel about this. We will access your situation, and we can keep people on that you like; we will keep the best of your staff and bring technology to increase their productivity.

We are not a high-pressure sales organization. . . . We just want you to make an informed decision.

Feel–felt–found. I know how you feel; you're not alone. A lot of people I work with felt the same way, but after they worked with us, they found Selling Team a perfect fit.

THE OPTOMETRIST!

Remember when you are at the optometrist? When you sit down in the chair and all of the equipment comes out and surrounds your head and you start looking through all of the lenses?

The doctor then says "better or worse" until you can't tell anymore. The same applies when you are hit with an objection or a brick wall (nontalker). "Mr. Prospect, I'm sure there is one thing that could make your business life better. Now what would that be?" "What would make things worse?" (Attempting to identify any potential risk)

Five after five strategy: We all know that the gatekeeper can be your friend or your nemesis. Make it a habit to call five prospects after 5:00 that you were unable to connect with throughout the day.

One great strategy to do is at the end the day, end with five calls to key prospects that either the gatekeeper blocked you or you were unable to connect with.

Do not leave another message if you had left one during the day.

ROAD MAP TO SUCCESS

Use this "tick" sheet to keep track of your progress throughout the day. Make sales into a game and have fun at it. This can also be used as a self-coaching tool to help you be more successful in your selling efforts. For example, if you're getting no one on the phone throughout the day, switch your calling times to before 9:00 a.m. or after 5:00 p.m. If you're having a lot of conversations and not closing for an appointment, record yourself and listen to your voice and identify your challenges.

Daily Sales Goals: _____ Date: _____

Dials: 100-99-98-97-96-95-94-93-92-91-90-89-88-87-86-85-84-83-82-81-80-79-78-77-76-75-74-73-72-71-70-69-68-67-66-65-64-63-62-61-60-59-58-57-56-55-54-53-52-51-50-49-48-47-46-45-44-43-42-41-40-39-38-37-36-35-34-33-32-31-30-29-28-27-26-25-24-23-22-21-20-19-18-17-16-15-14-13-12-11-10-09-08-07-06-05-04-03-02-01—Nice job!

Decision Makers:
20-19-18-17-16-15-14-13-12-11-10-09-08-07-06-05-04-03-02-01—Great job!

Face-to-Face Appointments:
3-2-1—Unbelievable superstar!!

E-mail addresses: (How many did you collect?)

20-19-18-17-16-15-14-13-12-11-10-09-08-07-06-05-04-03-02-01
—Awesome Job!

Positives: _____

Challenges: _____

Sales Pro Tips: Preparing for Your First Face-to-Face Call

1. Print out any relevant news article that contains social proof that what you are selling is relevant and solves a problem.
2. Dress for success; look and act like a professional. Your first impression is the only one that matters.
3. Be on time.
4. Be on their calendar. Send an electronic invite via e-mail to make sure it's on their calendar.

5. Be prepared with relevant questions that pertain to the prospect's problem or challenges.

6. Have a clear agenda in place to keep the meeting on time and engaging.

7. Compliment your prospect on any work they have done so far to solve the problem themselves.

8. Send out an executive summary of your meeting to the prospect and all parties at the meeting and not at the meeting.

9. Compliment on any work they have done so far to solve the problem themselves.

10. On the second appointment, ask them: "Has anything changed since we last spoke?" to open a dialogue and create a conversation.

11. Before presenting a proposal, revisit their problem areas by showing them again the areas you might have conducted in a past meeting or demonstration. Restate their challenges and your recommendations and ask: "Did I capture all of your current needs? Anything else you would like to add?" Always have agreements on your person, filled out and ready to present.

12. Send out a handwritten thank-you note after all first calls.

Questions to Ask on the First Call Include the Four Critical Elements in Any Sales Process

1. Pain/pleasure. What is your solution going to do to help them with their current challenges and make them happy?

2. Do you have the correct decision maker? Have you asked, "Walk me through your buying process"?

3. Budget. Have you asked about money and vetted any constraints?

4. When do they want the solution? Have you set realistic timetables?

   Pain _____

   DM _____

   Budget _____

   Completion Date _____

   Objectives: What would you like the end result to be?

How would things be different from now at the conclusion of the project?

Ideally, what three things must be accomplished?

How would you like to be known as a result of this project?

What must be changed, fixed, or improved the most?

Measures of success: How will you know these outcomes have been achieved?

What indices will you use to tell you that we're on the right track?

What current measures are you using that we can apply?

What measures should be created unique to this project?

Value: What will the outcomes mean to you and your organization?

How much improvement, conservatively, do you expect from a successful project?

What is it worth on an annualized basis and a longer-term basis?

What does this mean quantitatively and qualitatively?

Sample Pain Letter

Date

Name
Position
Company
Address
City, State, Zip

Dear [insert name]:

I am very glad we had the opportunity to meet and discuss the obstacles between XYZ Company's current (identified gap) and the effective, efficient process you seek to attain. Specifically, you shared your primary critical issues:

- Inability . . .
- Lack of . . .
- Absence of team cohesion
- Failure to meet . . .

- Insufficient plan to ensure stability in the face of internal change

We also discussed additional areas where Selling Team will provide XYZ Company supplemental value with our recommendations, guidance, and extensive referral network. These areas include (1) item A, (2) item B, and (3) item C.

As we move forward, please let me know if there is anything else we need to address.

In my experience a well-defined action plan promises the best results. Our agreed plan is as follows:

Selling Team:
- Action item 1: deliver proposal by date.
- Action item 2: discuss proposal and any necessary revisions by date.
- Action item 3: state additional action item and specifics.

XYZ Company:

Action item 1: review this letter and confirm key issues and focus areas.

Please let me convey my enthusiasm in giving you tangible, measurable results regarding XYZ Company's . . . [goal]. I will be in touch with you on [date] to discuss our next steps.

Respectfully,

CHAPTER 10

◆ ◆ ◆

YOUR SMART
PROSPECTING LAUNCH

◆ ◆ ◆

*Training is only the beginning of the learning process:
execution is everything.*

Mastering the art and science of prospecting to get that all-important first appointment will take you deeply into the sales process, your first date with a special person, and so much more.

I have trained hundreds of sales professionals in the process described in this book, and the results have been extraordinary. You can have the same types of results by simply following the process I outline in this book. There's no magic, just attention to detail and spending time acquainting yourself thoroughly with yourself, your prospect, and the prospect's company and its pain.

Continually practice thinking like a prospect rather than a sales professional. Put yourself in the prospect's shoes and think about what approach would best get your attention. Focus on what your prospects want, what their needs are, and how they like to be sold. And forget about yourself.

Make yourself a trusted advisor and consultant to your prospects and clients, not a salesperson.

Your needs, wants, and objectives should always be secondary if they are in evidence at all. If your needs (and in some instances desperation) are strapped to the front of you like a parachute, you (and your prospect) will have great difficulty ignoring your issues long enough to concentrate on the prospect. You won't fool the prospect or anyone else.

If you have been slowly sinking under the weight of those dreaded cold calls and first appointment approach calls, you have nothing to lose but a little time by trying my method.

I believe that you'll find it useful and productive and that it will help you capture more appointments than you ever thought possible.

Remember that the more people you see, the more money you will make. It's that simple.

To Your SALes Success!

Mike

APPENDIX A

SHARED TRAITS WORKSHEET

Date _____

Prospect _____   E-mail _____

Company _____   Opportunity _____

Phone _____   Next steps _____

SALES PROFESSIONAL		PROSPECT NAME	
Unique Traits	Shared behaviors and Learning Styles	Unique Traits

APPENDIX B

OPENING STATEMENT TEMPLATE

(Your name) _____

(Your company) _____

(Your phone number) _____

Benefit statement or pain (UVP) _____

_____

Company news reference or tie-in _____

What you are selling, in simple English (USP) _____

_____

Next steps _____

_____

_____

Invitation to contact you _____

_____

(Your name and telephone number again)

Conclusion _____

APPENDIX C

DAILY TIME MANAGEMENT LOG

DAILY TIME LOG

	Task/Activity What are your priorities today to move your business forward?	Total Time	Planned?	Value?	Objective
7:00 a.m.					
7:10 a.m.					
7:20 a.m.					
7:30 a.m.					
7:40 a.m.					
7:50 a.m.					
8:00 a.m.					
8:10 a.m.					
8:20 a.m.					
8:30 a.m.					
8:40 a.m.					

8:50 a.m.	9:00 a.m.	9:10 a.m.	9:20 a.m.	9:30 a.m.	9:40 a.m.	9:50 a.m.	10:00 a.m.	10:10 a.m.	10:20 a.m.	10:30 a.m.	10:40 a.m.	10:50 a.m.

Task/Activity What are your priorities today to move your business forward?	Total Time	Planned?	Value?	Objective
11:00 a.m.				
11:10 a.m.				
11:20 a.m.				
11:30 a.m.				
11:40 a.m.				
11:50 a.m.				
12:00 p.m.				
12:10 p.m.				
12:20 p.m.				
12:30 p.m.				
12:40 p.m.				
12:50 p.m.				

1:00 p.m.				
1:10 p.m.				
1:20 p.m.				
1:30 p.m.				
1:40 p.m.				
1:50 p.m.				
2:00 p.m.				
2:10 p.m.				
2:20 p.m.				
2:30 p.m.				
2:40 p.m.				
2:50 p.m.				
3:00 p.m.				

Task/Activity What are your priorities today to move your business forward?	Total Time	Planned?	Value?	Objective
3:10 p.m.				
3:20 p.m.				
3:30 p.m.				
3:40 p.m.				
3:50 p.m.				
4:00 p.m.				
4:10 p.m.				
4:20 p.m.				
4:30 p.m.				
4:40 p.m.				
4:50 p.m.				
5:00 p.m.				

5:10 p.m.	5:20 p.m.	5:30 p.m.	5:40 p.m.	5:50 p.m.	6:00 p.m.	6:10 p.m.	6:20 p.m.	6:30 p.m.	6:40 p.m.	6:50 p.m.	7:00 p.m.

PREPARING FOR TOMORROW:
ACTIONS: NEXT STEPS AND TO-DO LIST

APPENDIX D

SALES SENSE LETTER

sales Sense™
Solutions, Inc.

Sales Sense Letter Framework

Dear: _____

▶ **Question or grabber:**

What if _____, what would this mean to your business?
{you could achieve a 10 to 30 % increase in revenue or reduction in time or cost}

▶ **Result of using our services:**

Our clients have saved over _____ and _____ to the bottom line.
{10 to 20 % in time using our system, resulting in less turnover}   {adding 10 to 20 % in revenue}

Three critical areas separate_____ from all others:
{our company/product/service}

▶ **Unique Selling Proposition:**

- Unique value proposition:
    - ✓ I help (target) solve (key need/want) by (what you do).
- Why people buy from you:
    - ✓ Our best customers tell us they like _____.
- If you went out of business today, what customers would miss most:
    - ✓ and our _____ is why they keep buying from us year over year.

▶ **Testimonial from client, if you have approval:**

<name> of <company> wrote a letter to our president recently that mentioned: _____.
I will call you _____ to introduce myself and learn more about your business and (key need/want).

Respectfully,

<your name>
<company>
<contact information>

By taking a few moments to speak with me, you will receive _____ or the extension of an offer.

©2012 Sales Sense Solutions, Inc.

J. D. Brown

APPENDIX E

PROSPECT APPROACH PLANNING CHECKLIST

- ☐ Research and understand your target market, territory, and industry:
    - ☐ What does your target market value about you and your company?
    - ☐ How can you communicate most effectively with your target market?
- ☐ Understand your own personal behavior and learning style
- ☐ Evaluate this prospect's personal behavior and learning style
- ☐ In the context of this prospect, develop, review, or update:
    - ☐ Your unique selling proposition (USP)
    - ☐ Your unique value proposition (UVP)
- ☐ Create and commit to your sales goals for this specific prospect
- ☐ Develop your appointment messaging for this prospect:
    - ☐ Opening statement:
        - ☐ Voice mail
        - ☐ Live call
        - ☐ E-mail
    - ☐ Attention-getting benefit:
        - ☐ Voice mail
        - ☐ Live call
        - ☐ E-mail

☐ Design your approach to this prospect:
   ☐ Find contact information for:
      ☐ Prospect
      ☐ Gatekeeper
   ☐ Write out your scripts for this prospect:
      ☐ Voice mail
      ☐ Live call
      ☐ E-mail
☐ Make your call or write and send your e-mail
☐ Update CRM
☐ Use Postcall Evaluation (Appendix G) to evaluate how you did

APPENDIX F

PRECALL CHECKLIST

- [ ] Research the account before the call:
    - [ ] Company website
    - [ ] Journals and newspapers: recent articles, reviews, interviews
    - [ ] Industry information and company involvement
    - [ ] LinkedIn profiles and connections
    - [ ] Google search on the company name
- [ ] Learn the person's concerns in the business, DiSC style, personality, personal interests:
    - [ ] LinkedIn
    - [ ] Google search on the prospect's name
    - [ ] Mutual connections
    - [ ] Professional associations
- [ ] Send an agenda to the prospect at least two days before the meeting
- [ ] Appropriately dress for this call with this prospect:
    - [ ] Clean, pressed clothes (no dandruff, fuzz, dog or cat hair)
    - [ ] Shined shoes
    - [ ] Hair, face, and nails groomed
    - [ ] Mint, gum, or mouthwash for breath (dispose of gum before call)
    - [ ] Relax, stand up straight, and smile
- [ ] Be prepared with one to three benefits that correspond to the prospect's concerns and/or pain

☐ Practice your presentation beforehand
☐ Get organized, with all relevant information:
    ☐ Business cards
    ☐ Laptop with presentations
    ☐ Brochures
    ☐ Approved customer references
    ☐ Social media links for testimonials
☐ Print and bring extra agendas
☐ Have pens and a notebook for taking notes
☐ Remember the gatekeeper's name
☐ Fill out any contracts or forms in advance so that all you need is a signature
☐ Have your business agenda clearly defined for yourself:
    ☐ Complete picture of your sales process with this prospect in mind
    ☐ Your progress goal for this call
    ☐ What information you need to learn during the call
    ☐ The next steps after the call:
        ☐ For your prospect
        ☐ For you
        ☐ Timing of the next steps

APPENDIX G

POSTCALL EVALUATION

PERSONAL PERFORMANCE EVALUATION

- ☐ You reviewed the meeting's purpose briefly to get started.
- ☐ You mentioned something related to the prospect's company or industry early in the meeting.
- ☐ You read the prospect's body language to gauge trust and rapport.
- ☐ You requested the prospect's permission to ask more questions and record or take notes on the answers.
- ☐ You asked questions in a conversational, casual manner.
- ☐ You targeted questions well to understand real concerns and needs.
- ☐ You kept the focus on the prospect's pain.
- ☐ You briefly mentioned relevant products or solutions that addressed the prospect's concerns, needs, and pain.
- ☐ You addressed any objections raised.
- ☐ You offered customer testimonials and social media links.
- ☐ You provided the prospect with customer contact information.
- ☐ You requested a commitment to the next step.

What could you have done better in the meeting?

_____

_____

What will you do differently with this prospect next time?

_____

_____

_____

_____

What will you do differently with every prospect next time?

_____

_____

_____

MEETING OUTCOMES

☐ Here are the desired outcomes of the call:
  - ☐ Got a better understanding of the prospect's objectives and perspective
  - ☐ Got a better understanding of the benefits the customer wants
  - ☐ Established permission to progress to the next step of the sales process
  - ☐ Took care of any action items for which you are responsible
  - ☐ Sent a handwritten thank-you note immediately to the prospect and a separate thank you to the gatekeeper, if appropriate
  - ☐ Updated CRM

APPENDIX H

CALL SCRIPT WORKSHEETS

FIND THE DECISION MAKER SCRIPT

Hello, this is _____ *from [your company] [Gatekeeper's name], could you please tell me who is the person who makes decisions about* _____ *?*

> *Would you mind spelling that for me, please?*
> *What is [prospect name's] title?* _____
> *What is the best time to reach him or her?* _____
> *Could you give me his or her e-mail address?* _____
> *Does he or she have a direct phone number or an extension?* _____
> *I have his or her office address as* _____ *.*
> *Is that correct? Is there a mail stop or floor number I should add?*

DECISION MAKER CALL SCRIPT: FIRST CALL

Hi, [gatekeeper's name]. This is _____ *from [your company]. Is* _____ *in? Could I speak with him [or her] for just a minute?*

(If gatekeeper says: "Yes, he [or she] is expecting your call.")

Decision maker picks up the line.

Mr. D-M, I'm [your name] from [your company]. I'm calling to introduce myself and learn more about your (point of pain) and talk about how we might work together, increase your efficiency, and decrease your costs. (pause briefly)
Is this a good time for a quick five-minute conversation? Great.

(If it is not good, set a time for a return call. Follow up with an e-mail to confirm the call.)

Can you tell me a little about your business and your goals?

_____

_____

_____

_____

Then be quiet, listen, and take notes, clarifying any unclear points quickly. Do *not* launch into a sales pitch now, as it's not appropriate and you're not ready.

I'd like to send you some information about our solutions for your (point of pain and challenges), then touch base in a couple of days to see when we might get together. (pause for two beats) Are you currently in the market for [products/services/solutions] like ours?

_____

_____

I have your address as [street, city, state, zip] and your name as _____ [spell it, even easy ones] and your title as _____. Is that correct?
Thank you for taking time out of your busy day to speak with me. I'll get that information in the mail to you today.
Have a great day! Good-bye.

DECISION MAKER CALL SCRIPT: FOLLOW-UP TO PACKET CALL

Hi, [gatekeeper's name]. This is _____ *from [your company]. Is* _____ *in? Could I please speak with him [or her] for just a minute?*

(If gatekeeper says, "Yes, he [or she] is expecting your call.")

Mr. D-M, this is [your name] from [company]. Have you received our information packet on [solution] to [their point of pain]? _____ *Have you looked at it?* _____

Yes, the person has looked over the packet. Give the prospect a second or so to get it and to add any comments or observations he or she may have rather than jumping immediately to the next step. Listening throughout these steps is invaluable. Make notes about the prospect's comments.

_____

_____

_____

_____

_____

_____

_____

What questions can I answer for you?

Answer the prospect's questions. If you don't know, say so and promise to get to the prospect within a day with the answer. Then move to one of the alternative conclusions that follow.

_____

_____

_____

_____

_____

_____

CONCLUSION 1

Well, when could we get together briefly so I can show you more about how [our product/service/solution] can [cure your pain or solve your issues]?

> *Would Tuesday or Wednesday be better?* _____
>
> *Would morning or afternoon work better?*_____
>
> *How about* [give them two times to choose from]:
>
> *9:30 a.m. or 11:00 a.m.* _____?
>
> *2:00 p.m. or 3:30 p.m.* _____?

Thank you so much, Mr. or Ms. Decision Maker. I really appreciate your time today, and I'm looking forward to seeing you [repeat the time, day, and date]. Have a great day.

CONCLUSION 2

Prospect didn't have a chance to look at the packet:

> *While we're on the phone, let's open the packet and go through it quickly together so I can answer your questions.*

Walk the prospect through the packet briefly. Answer the prospect's questions. If you don't know, say so and promise to get back to the prospect within a day with the answer. Then move on to set the appointment.

> *Well, when could we get together briefly so I can show you more about how [our product/service/solution] can [cure your pain or solve your issues]?*
>
> *Would Tuesday or Wednesday be better?* _____
>
> *Would morning or afternoon work better?*_____
>
> *How about* [give them two times to choose from]:
>
> *9:30 a.m. or 11:00 a.m.* _____?
>
> *2:00 p.m. or 3:30 p.m.* _____?

Thank you so much, Mr. or Ms. Decision Maker. I really appreciate your time today, and I'm looking forward to seeing you [repeat the time, day, and date]. Have a great day.

Prospect didn't get the packet:

I'm so sorry; let me send another to you. (Or send it by courier if feasible.)

[Confirm the prospect's address one more time] _____

_____

_____

I'll call you back _____ *when you have received the packet. Again, my apologies. Have a great day.*

APPENDIX I

SMART PROSPECTING THAT WORKS EVERY TIME! BOOK EVALUATION

We sincerely hope that you have found *Smart Prospecting That Works Every Time!* helpful in your personal quest for more prospects, appointments, and sales.

Please take a few moments to provide some feedback so that we can make this product more useful and more convenient for you and your fellow sales professionals. Please send us your thoughts on the following questions in an e-mail to mike@SalesSenseSolutions.com:

What did you find most helpful about this book?
What would have helped you use this book more productively?
What could we do better with this book in the future?

Thank you!

CALL ME

If you are having difficulty zeroing in on your target market, give me a call so that we can discuss what additional resources might help you uncover the golden prospects you seek.

How to reach me: If you want to contact me directly, call (585) 704-6453 or e-mail mike@salessensesolutions.com. If you want to do some exploring on your own, please visit www.SalesSenseSolutions.com, www.Smart-Prospecting.com, and www.MDKrause.com.

Sales Sense Solutions offers the following resources to help you in your quest for sales sense and SMART Prospecting solutions:

- *Speaking engagements.* Here is a way for you to sample our sales strategy motivation and instruction before committing to something bigger. From negotiating to ethical selling, we offer a variety of topics.
- *Comprehensive, high-performance sales systems and services.* We handle everything from initial measurement, to sales staff evaluations, to strategic sales education. Whatever your sales-related needs are, we can handle them in a way that puts time and money in your organization's pocket.
- *Four-hour sales checkup.* We've designed this checkup for those who know that they want help but aren't sure where to start. This service package is an easy-to-start, priced-to-please, quick-to-finish solution for new clients.[1]
- *Hiring assessments.* If you want to hire top-quality sales representatives efficiently and confidently, Sales Sense Solutions can provide the accessible experience and skill set you need to make it happen at a price you can afford.
- *Social media solutions.* A turnkey solution puts this powerful sales and lead generation channel to work for your organization. It includes personalized instruction so that you can manage it on your own in just a few minutes a day.

Here is a quick guide to the rules of engagement in case you're hesitant about giving me a call for assistance:

1. *All* information will be held in confidentiality; if desired, I will sign your nondisclosure agreement.
2. I'm looking to partner with you and your team.
3. I promise you that at the end of our meeting we will at a minimum know a little more about each other.

NOTES

Chapter 1

1. Anna H. Spencer, PhD, Infinity Institute, http://www.infinityinst .com/articles/know_thyself.html, retrieved May 12, 2011.
2. Inscape Publishing. Used with permission, http://www.inscape publishing.com.
3. Inscape Publishing, Everything DiSC® Sales Profile and DiSC® Classic. Used with permission, http://www.inscapepublishing.com; http://www.everythingdisc.com; http://www.discclassic.com.
4. Ibid.
5. www.BusinessBalls.com, ©David Kolb; original concept relating to Kolb's learning styles model and Alan Chapman 2003–2010 review and code and diagrams artwork. http://www.businessballs.com/kolblearn ingstyles.htm. Reprinted with permission. Retrieved June 15, 2011.
6. Hayden Louring, Ehow contributor, http://www.ehow.com/ facts_5179201_four-learning_styles.html, retrieved June 15, 2011.

Chapter 2

1. Napoleon Hill, InspirationalSpark.com, retrieved June 14, 2011, from http://www.inspiiationalspark.com/goal-quotes.html.
2. http://www.thelastlecture.com/aboutbk.htm, retrieved September 12, 2011.
3. http://www.merriam-webster.com/dictionary/goal, retrieved April 19, 2011.
4. Ibid.
5. http://www.212movie.com, retrieved April 19, 2011.
6. http://www.helpguide.org/mental/stress_management_relief_coping .htm, retrieved April 20, 2011.

7. Mayo Clinic, http://www.mayoclinic.health/positive-thinking/
   SR00009, retrieved April 26, 2011.
8. Mayo Clinic, http://www.mayoclinic.health/positive-thinking/
   SR00009, retrieved April 26, 2011.

Chapter 3

1. Thomas Paine, http://www.ushistory.org/paine/crisis/c-01.htm,
   retrieved April 20, 2011.
2. http://www.volvo.com/group/volvosplash-global/en-gb/volvo_splash.
   htm, retrieved April 20, 2011.

Chapter 4

1. U.S. Small Business Administration, http://web.sba.gov/faqs/faqindex
   .cfm?areaID=24, retrieved September 14, 2011.
2. U.S. Census Bureau, http://www.census.gov, accessed April 18, 2011.
3. www.manta.com, accessed April 18, 2011.
4. http://www.marketingsource.com/directories/associations/us accessed
   April 18, 2011.

Chapter 5

1. http://www.marketingsherpa.com/article.php?ident=31674, retrieved
   June 6, 2011. Used by permission.

Chapter 6

1. http://www.careerbuilder.com/share/aboutus/pressreleasesdetail.aspx?
   id=pr519andsd=8%2f19%2f2009anded=12%2f31%2f2009andsiteid
   =cbprandsc_cmpl=cb_pr519_, retrieved June 7, 2011.

Chapter 7

1. Sally McGhee, McGhee Productivity Solutions, http://www.microsoft
   .com/atwork/productivity/email.aspx, retrieved July 26, 2011.

2. 7 Steps to Jump-Start Your Email Marketing Strategy, © HubSpot .com, http://www.hubspot.com/7-steps-to-jump-start-your-email -marketing-strategy, retrieved May 25, 2011.
3. http://www.Gladwell.com/blink/, retrieved August 22, 2011.
4. www.google.com/alerts, retrieved August 9, 2011.
5. *Plain Language at Work* newsletter, May 15, 2005, number 15, "What's with the Newspapers?" http://www.impact-information.com/ impactinfo/newsletter/plwork15.htm, retrieved June 16, 2011.
6. Eric S. Raymond, http://www.catb.org/jargon/html/F/FUD.html, retrieved June 16, 2011.

Chapter 8

1. Larry Weber, *Marketing to the Social Web: How Digital Customer Communities Build Your Business,* 2d ed., Wiley, 2009.
2. Tom Atkinson and Ron Koprowski, "Sales Reps' Biggest Mistakes," *Harvard Business Review,* July–August 2006. Reprint F0607C, reprinted with permission.

Appendix I

1. http://salessensesolutions.com/How-Sales-Check-Up/4-hour-sales -check-up.html, accessed January 11, 2011.

INDEX

ABOUT THE AUTHOR

Mike Krause knows the challenges sales leaders and business professionals face every day, having sold well over $100 million in products and services in his twenty years of professional sales, consistently achieving high levels of success in sales, management and training. He is a seasoned veteran of driving and achieving quantifiable results across a wide array of business models and organization sizes.

Since running his first lemonade stand at the age of seven, Mike's proven approach to sales is to roll up his sleeves, jump into the trenches with his client's salespeople and do whatever it takes to teach them his customized tools, tactics and strategies to generate income and strengthen positive branding.

From building a landscape company from inception to 130 accounts in two years to being recognized as a top producer in each of the Fortune 500 companies for which he worked, Mike always exceeds his goals. Mike funded his undergraduate education at St. Bonaventure University with his landscaping company and later obtained a Master's degree in Strategic Leadership with a concentration in entrepreneurship from Roberts Wesleyan College.

After spending over twelve years in Corporate America, Mike discovered his true passion in helping business leaders and sales professionals achieve their sales objectives more rapidly through his highly effective selling processes. His previous book, *Sell or Sink: Strategies, Tactics and Tools Every Business Leader Must Know to Stay Afloat!* is available online through Amazon and Barnes & Noble.

Today, Mike Krause is the president and founder of Sales Sense Solutions, Inc. where he delivers measurable results with his clients using Fortune 500 strategies, tactics, and tools. The company's mission is to customize Fortune 500 sales experience and success systems for small and mid-sized companies. In addition to his thriving consulting work, Krause is an in-demand speaker and has received numerous awards for his acclaimed training programs. In his spare time, Mike enjoys piloting his sailboat on the Great Lakes, having successfully earned his marine captain's license three years ago.